# EXPECT DELAYS

## How To Reclaim Your Life, Light and Soul After Trauma

Dr. Danielle Delaney, Th.D., D.D.

Cover photo of Billboard/Banner Photography by Jon Abeyta
City & Road Signs photography by Danielle Delaney and Delangerous Productions
Billboard on Sunset Boulevard by OUTFRONT MEDIA
Additional graphics provided by www.shutterstock.com

www.ExpectDelaysBook.com

First published in 2017

Library of Congress Cataloging-in-Publication Data is available upon request.

Printed in the United States and Canada

ISBN: 978-1-77277-134-3

10-10-10 Publishing
Markham, Ontario
Canada

# Contents

# DEDICATION

*I dedicate this book to each and every person subjected to trauma beyond their control.*

*If you hear nothing else, hear that it is not your fault.*
*I survived; so will you.*

*These words are for you.*

# FOREWORD

Dr. Danielle Delaney, Th.D. is beyond passionate about guiding you through the dramatically difficult territory of healing from trauma. She has extensive expertise from living through rape and crisis herself, as well as being extraordinarily trained and experienced and at the very top upper echelon of practitioners in the fields of Trauma Recovery, Spiritual Counseling, and Addiction Aftercare. Dr. Delaney teaches with compassion, guides with her whole heart and her soul, and, through *Expect Delays,* she will help you on your spiritual path to finding your way back to yourself by showing you how she did it herself.

Dr. Delaney's personal journey has shown her the pitfalls encountered in healing from violence. She takes you through her own harrowing experience of trauma, and also shares with you a unique perspective as both a Survivor *and* a Counselor, guiding you with strategies to overcome your own trauma.

Dr. Delaney explains and shares with you why you *should* indeed expect delays in your personal recovery, and why it is desirable to embrace them as part of your journey. She speaks to you with respect and understanding, and from the vantage point of having been through it personally, using her philosophies and techniques for you to rise like a phoenix from the ashes. Do not delay in reclaiming your life or in utilizing the wisdom to open the door to your own healing; this book is the key to unlocking the door to your recovery!

I endorse Dr. Delaney and highly recommend for you to learn from her wisdom by reading this book. *Expect Delays* is a must-read for you, given that you have experienced different levels of trauma in your own life, or you love others who have. Dr. Delaney is simply ***dazzling*** with her writing style, and with her care, empathy and expertise. Do not miss out on reading this book!

Raymond Aaron
New York Times Bestselling Author

# Praise for Dr. Danielle Delaney and EXPECT DELAYS

"*Expect Delays* should be required reading for anyone coping with a traumatic experience or attempting to help a loved one or patient to do so. Dr. Danielle Delaney has obviously been there and holds the roadmap to healing with your soul intact. The manner in which Danielle explains that delays are to be expected, embraced and turned into strengths is unusually concise and intuitive. Perhaps because she has been there herself, Danielle knows the territory better than the rest, and in a way that others armed with even the best book learning of this area of expertise could ever hope for...there is no substitute for living, breathing life experience. Accept no substitute.

Danielle bravely fought for her life more than once, and continues to come out on top. Fortunately for her patients, she came through the other side and is now a living example of how to dance gracefully back into the spotlight of your own life. I am duly impressed. Expect to be both disarmed and charmed by Delaney and by 'Expect Delays,' as was I. Both Dr. Danielle Delaney and her story of tenacious survival and sheer will against the odds are entirely worthy of your full attention. Nobody does it better. I should know...I happen to be her proud father.

Brava!"

Dr. Richard Allen Williams, M.D., FACC, FAHA, FACP
**117th President, National Medical Association**
Clinical Professor of Medicine, UCLA School of Medicine
**Founder, Association of Black Cardiologists**
President/CEO, Minority Health Institute, Inc.
**Named "Ethnic Physician of the Year," California Medical Association Foundation**
Named a Local Hero by KCET TV and Union Bank
**Distinguished International Humanitarian Awardee, National Council of Women of the United States**
Lifesaver Award, American Heart Association, 2014

*Dr. Danielle Delaney, Th.D., D.D.*

October 8, 2012

To Whom it May Concern:

Danielle Delaney was the victim of random violent crimes in both 2005 and 2007, from which she suffered serious injuries. In addition to physical assault and rape, she was the victim of identity theft and was forced to relocate immediately for her own safety, since her attackers now possessed her personal information, contact numbers and addresses of her family, friends and colleagues. Law enforcement officials felt she and her close family and friends could suffer witness intimidation and further violence if she remained in her residence and neighborhood.

Ms. Delaney worked diligently for years to rehabilitate her leg injuries and regain her ability to walk. The traumatic brain injury she suffered in the attack was seriously debilitating, and it took some time for her to regain her physical and mental health. She suffered for years with both Post Traumatic Stress Disorder and Rape Trauma Syndrome.

Despite these tremendous challenges, Ms. Delaney became an advocate for victims of violent crime. She became a Certified Court Advocate, and returned to school to earn her Certification as a Crisis Counselor in order to help others. She now works with individuals in Aftercare in the field of Addiction & Recovery, assisting people in all forms of crises, working with rape survivors and adults molested as children. Ms. Delaney counsels individuals and guides them through the justice system as they reach for both recovery and resolution of legal issues.

Ms. Delaney has proven herself an asset to the City and County of Los Angeles. She has chosen to help others rather than remaining a passive victim, and guides others in seeing that they, too, can overcome their personal trials. Any employment interruptions or delays in bill payment for Ms. Delaney were due entirely to her injuries and forced relocation. The perpetrators of the crimes against Ms. Delaney, including any fraud against her bank accounts, are the fault of her attackers, and should not prevent her from re-establishing previously earned credit standing. Victims of violent crimes should not be required by any corporation or public utility to "start over" to prove her creditworthiness. Ms. Delaney deserves the chance to begin her financial life again without suffering further harm after her lengthy recovery. Official police reports should provide adequate evidence for offering special consideration, without crime victims being re-traumatized by having to repeatedly re-live the violence and aftermath that were always beyond their individual control.

Please use the information in this letter to seek appropriate measures to provide Ms. Delaney with necessary assistance.

Sincerely,

Deanna Tryon
dtryon@ceo.lacounty.gov

X

"As a psychotherapist in private practice specializing in recovery, I have been collaborating with Danielle for over 5 years. She is my go-to sober coach/companion provider/crisis management counselor and interventionist for clients in need of extra support. She possesses a unique skill set that combines being both supportive and motivational. I am grateful for her work with my clients and for the services that she provides."

**Noah Rothschild, LMFT, Transformational Psychotherapy**
**www.noahrothschild.com**

"Dr. Danielle Delaney is successful in what she does because she does it from her heart. She is driven to help those in need of trauma counseling, who are in need of intervention from drug or alcohol abuse, and she helps to assist and to pair those in need of accompaniment with one of her company's Sober Companions. That's not all. Danielle has a talk and radio show ("The Real Deal With Danielle Delaney "on VoiceAmerica) that helps to educate so many people around the world on various topics regarding addiction, mental health, and clinical psychology. Her passion is transparent and working with her is an absolute delight. Dr. Delaney is extremely educated in her field and knows how to best help those in need of crisis therapy. During the time that I have worked with Danielle, I've seen her help many people from all across the globe and bring them to Passages, where they have been treated and healed to go on and live a life free from addiction. It is because of Danielle & DDC, Inc.'s dedication that many people who once struggled with trauma and addiction, no longer have to do so. She is on a wonderful mission and it's truly beautiful to see all that she's doing in helping to improve the lives of others."

**Jennifer McDougall**
**Digital Marketing | Social Media Manager | PR**
**Passages Malibu**

"My recommendation of Dr. Danielle Delaney is written with the highest form of truth and integrity. It is needless to say, Dr. Delaney has been through experiences which many of us may only imagine. Most individuals would succumb to darkness and despair if they went through what she has endured.

However, she's managed to secure her strength, courage, and valor with such grace that she's now helping thousands of women and girls who've been traumatized, abused, and raped. She hosts her very well-received show on VoiceAmerica, which reaches millions of individuals worldwide.

Her expertise in crisis intervention, therapy and healing is priceless and invaluable to countless individuals who've suffered extensive trauma. It is safe to say our world is a much better place because of Dr. Delaney and her service to our people.

I provide Dr. Delaney my highest form of respect and recommendation, with no reservation or hesitation whatsoever. If any of you who read this wish to receive more details about my experience with Dr. Delaney, I encourage you to contact me freely."

**Rajiv Uttamchandani, Astrophysicist, Professor, Human Rights Activist, Founder & Chairman at ISSHR, Founder & President at H.E.R.**

"Danielle's ability to understand all aspects of the human experience with the utmost empathy, understanding and kindness is what makes her an amazing counselor, specialist and healer. She gives every individual she works with her very best, getting to know them intimately, and she tailors their healthy living plan to meet their individual needs. She walks the walk, and has helped so many people recover, thrive and heal."

**Erica Spiegelman, CADACII, Addiction Specialist, Counselor, Speaker & Author of "Rewired: A Bold New Approach to Addiction and Recovery"**

"I've been working with Danielle for almost 5 years now. She has been such a pleasure to work with. Danielle is especially thoughtful, and always on the ball when dealing with her clients. Danielle is extremely honest about how she can be most effective in each situation, and honesty is very important when dealing with our population. Her intervention skills and her manner of speaking with her clients in crisis situations are top notch. I'm lucky to walk with her in this industry."

**Ross Remien, Owner at Rebos Treatment Center**

"I have had the pleasure of working alongside Danielle Delaney for about 5 years now. I cannot recommend her enough! In these 5 years, I've seen her engaged in deeply meaningful and powerful work with her clients in the field of mental health counseling, sober coaching, and trauma and crisis work. I have experienced firsthand the work she has done, the people she has touched, and the success stories she has helped to create. The most beautiful thing is it is done with a deep sense of spirit, warmth, empathy, dedication, and intuition that one does not see very often in this line of work. Danielle is able to reach her clients at that soul level, and assist each individual in creating lasting change... and she has this way about her, this charisma, that makes the process truly enjoyable! She clearly demonstrates this mastery with her clients, but also imparts this energy and vision in connecting with her colleagues, business acquaintances, and others who cross her path. This rare mix of empathy, humor, sensitivity, spirit, and ambition sets a great example for the rest us, and explains why everyone loves working with Danielle no matter what role they play in her life!

I cannot recommend Danielle highly enough, and I have only optimistic predictions for your future with her! Thank you for taking the time to read this, and best wishes along your path. Blessings!"

**Christopher Scott Pearson, Marriage and Family Psychotherapist Intern (MFTI#88052)/Certified Mental Health Counselor/Life Coach**

"Danielle Delaney is a highly regarded person in her industry. This work is her passion, and she is uniquely dedicated. It is her experience as well as her personal touch and style in helping others that will always set her apart from, and well above, the rest.

Her availability and mobility as a Concierge Counselor are a huge asset, as she is able to travel where she is needed and be physically present. Some of the life experiences that she has endured, and which have shaped her world, have made her that much stronger, and that much more compelling as an expert at helping others to heal in various ways. As a professional colleague and friend, I am struck by her integrated professionalism and compassion. She truly impacts individuals in a way that is multi faceted, and that demonstrates her commitment and willingness to go the extra mile to transform lives.

Observing her as a Sober Coach and Counselor, Crisis Counselor and Th.D, I will not hesitate to recommend her as Best In Show in her field. Danielle is a person who will stop at nothing to facilitate her clients to higher purpose and performance. Her volunteer interests and past experience highlight her stellar abilities. Dr. Delaney is a compelling speaker and writer, with outstanding credentials and a spotless track record in guiding others in making sense of the chaotic world around them."

**Christina Adams, Staff Nurse at Fort Sanders Regional Medical Center**

**Radio MD & Rewired Radio Show "Drug-Assisted Rape: A Disturbing Trend on the Rise" brings kudos from RadioMD editor**
**Sexual Assault: A Crisis Sweeping the Nation**

"A few weeks ago, I watched a video of Lady Gaga's song, "Til It Happens to You," and I was incredibly moved.

And angry. And really, really sad.

It's an extremely powerful video that shows the devastating effects of sexual assault. I immediately downloaded the song, and now, whenever it pops up in my playlist, I am reminded of how relevant this issue is in our current society.

From the increasing number of assaults on college campuses, to the aftermath and disgusting details of celebrities like Bill Cosby and Darren Sharper, there's no denying that this disturbing trend needs to be addressed, and soon. Let's not forget the shocking promotional efforts of Bloomingdale's, with its print campaign saying: "Spike your best friend's eggnog when they're not looking."

What the WHAT?

Guest of Rewired Radio, Dr. Danielle Delaney, knows firsthand how debilitating sexual assault can be, as she was a victim herself. She is now a rape crisis counselor, and recently joined host Erica Spiegelman to share some information about sexual assault and drug-assisted rape.

First, an infuriating statistic: over 15,000 cases of drug-assisted rape are seen in ERs every year... and that's probably not even half of the actual cases. Drug-assisted rape is extremely difficult to prove, and oftentimes the lack of knowledge or resources in the ER can only add to the disbelief.

The substances that are used are odorless and tasteless. Even if you're not drinking alcohol, your beverage can be compromised. Don't put faith in the integrity of the bartender, either. They often get paid to do a patron's dirty work... which is what happened to me once in New York. Fortunately, I had my husband with me, and he kept me safe.

Never accept a drink from someone you don't know (or someone you don't trust). And, trust your gut. It's sometimes the one thing that will prevent you from getting into a bad situation. As Danielle puts it, you don't want to be saying "I knew it, I knew it..." but rather "I know it."

If you have been a victim, there are people who can help... people like Danielle. But, make sure you specifically ask for a rape counselor, as not every therapist is skilled in these types of crises. You will suffer from triggers at different times throughout the year and in different situations, so it's important to have a counselor who can help you navigate that. If you know someone who has been assaulted, Danielle says the most important thing you can do is to believe them.

Dr. Danielle Delaney has such great information on this topic; as I said, much of it firsthand knowledge. I encourage you to take a listen to the segment, whether you're male or female, young or old. No one is immune from the impact of sexual assault."

**Sylvia Anderson, Editor, RadioMD**

"The first time I met Danielle, I was immediately captured by her positive energy. Having not known her full story, I was captivated by the absolute tenacity she possesses. Alternatively, she, not knowing much about me, drew out facets of my life in such an empathetic and compassionate way.

Now that I know Danielle a little better, I've come to realize just how valuable she is in her life's work. She is likely the most highly intelligent, driven and motivating individual I've met. Whether she's speaking to the masses or one-on-one, Danielle's message is one of love, hope, kindness and survival."

**Sylvia Anderson, RadioMD Editor in Chief, RadioMD Producer**

"I am pleased to write a recommendation for Danielle Delaney's work as a Certified Crisis Interventionist, Rape Crisis Counselor, and Addiction Specialist. This one is easy. Danielle is the best that I have ever seen in my 55 years of practicing medicine, period. I could go on and on about how compassionate, supportive, uplifting, considerate, and persistent she is, but there really is no need to embellish her profile any further. She is a shining star who breaks through the cloudy skies of despair that her clients often face, and it is no wonder that her brilliant efforts are so frequently successful in helping to extract them from their misery. More needs to be shared about this gifted lady and her talents. Those who seek her services are very fortunate to utilize them."

**Dr. Richard Allen Williams, MD, FACC, President/CEO, Minority Health Institute, Inc.**

"Dr. Danielle Delaney has counseled me regarding my being assaulted. She worked with me on Skype, over the telephone, and also came to my home when my PTSD did not allow me to leave the house. I read an article about her extraordinary high IQ of 156 on the Stanford-Binet, the top two percentile which I study, and so I was really intrigued to meet her. She has a depth of understanding that is unparalleled. I went to therapists and psychiatrists and support groups that offered far less knowledge and support than Danielle did; she really knows what she is talking about, was able to discuss my fears and impulses with me in a way that other professionals and doctors simply could not. She also stressed treatment that does not involve medicating myself unnecessarily, and referred me to a Post-Traumatic

Stress Disorder specialist and to a naturopath to help me with my physical health issues which she believed may stem from the assault, something the other doctors and shrinks NEVER figured out. Since my first few sessions with her, I find that I am indeed reclaiming my life, and finding some peace. I recommend her highly – unlike others, she brings her personal experience with crime/rape to the table, even gives advice as a court advocate. I would refer anyone that I know dealing with rape or molestation issues to her, without a second thought. Best doctor/therapist/counselor that I have ever seen, hands down. Worth the cost, which I found to be a competitive and fair rate."

**Juliette S.**

"Danielle has saved my life not once but twice. I was referred to her as a crisis interventionist and counselor. Initially she assisted me as a sober companion during a difficult time, from a rehab facility in CA to my home and back. Then, she came to me as I had subsequent struggles and assisted me with guided care in my home after I relapsed a few times. She provided me with care, guidance and security while I was going through a difficult time. She is easy and comfortable to be around and, of course, completely nonjudgmental, having walked this path herself. She is an expert in her field and devoted to changing lives for the better I am so thankful that she helped to change mine!"

**Kim Moger, Aflac Regional Sales Coordinator and Talent Acquisition**

"My experience with being in treatment with Dr. Danielle Delaney has been life-saving.

She has come through when & where others are totally unavailable, and it is not for lack of work or that she has any sort of "extra" time she is always on the go and she is under tremendous pressure, but she stops and MAKES the time when others don't; and is clear, concise, and supportive when I need her. NEVER have I had a doctor or therapist/counselor on whom I could count to be so steady and so helpful to me at any hour of need in the manner that she has been. This unusual courtesy has been extended to my entire family. She has been a liaison to people in my life when we needed her desperately. I have looked to her guidance through untimely deaths of loved ones, several of my own health crises, and in emergencies. I can't imagine how she manages to do it all and run her practice and her companies. She makes things beyond comfortable & I feel soothed and at ease in her presence, and because of the depth of her own personal experience with trauma, I feel more safely understood by her than by others, as well as in knowing that she is invested in my healing and clearly shows her care for me.

She is well-trained and highly educated most certainly, but I find that her natural instincts with her patients as well are absolutely second to none.

Dr. Danielle Delaney faithfully & repeatedly DAZZLED me & my family with her level of care. Whether rushing to my side during illness & hospitalization and taking charge, or taking a midnight family session, she has never made me feel like an inconvenience. Rather, I've felt nothing but honesty and deep respect emanating from her.

I can say with sincerity I'd not be where I am in my life today if not for Danielle's cautious care with me. Her book "Expect Delays" about reclaiming your soul after trauma will help to heal and to save so many from harm. I have no doubt that Danielle's star will continue to rise and to brightly shine. Consider yourself extremely lucky if you are holding this book in your hands.

With deepest gratitude,"

**Syd Wilder**

## Dr. Danielle Delaney, Th.D., D.D.

"Danielle Delaney was my Court Advocate for my rape case, in which my rapist was caught after a decade and I had to fly from another country to the U.S. to be in court.

Danielle knows her areas of expertise extremely well, from her extensive training in Rape Crisis as well as her work with victims of violent crime, and her own personal experience. She dressed the part for the courtroom, worked with my detective prior to and during the case in order to be a liaison for me for my case, and was on time bright and early to help me and to lend an ear and accompany me to the courthouse. I had to see this predator who had altered my life forever again in person, and she was a wonderful support to me. While I was on the stand I felt badgered, being forced to relive what had happened and answer painful questions from the defense. When Danielle noticed any distress in my voice or appearance, she would stand up and ask to remove her client (me) from the stand for a moment, and would step outside with me and would kindly, patiently, objectively and calmly explain to me that this line of questioning was to prove the kidnap portion of the crime, which would add additional years to the rapist's prison sentence. She was able to calm me and to soothe my nerves enough for me to go in and continue what I was there to do... to testify on my own behalf. Afterward, she treated me to a healthy lunch so that I could debrief with her, and drove me back to my hotel room and called to check in on me later, knowing intuitively that the experience was rattling to the core. They even ticketed her car at the meter as she took me out to lunch and as rattled as I was, she was as cool as a cucumber the entire time with her eyes only on what mattered, impossible to distract.

It was a beyond stressful and surreal once-in-a-lifetime day with so much mixed emotion coming from me, and Danielle handled it all with grace. As a Doctor, Counselor and a Court Advocate, I cannot recommend Danielle Delaney more highly.

I see why she is so well regarded in her industry of Counseling Psychology and Addiction Aftercare. She has a manner that is firm but very kind, and a work ethic that is truly grace under pressure, never forgetting even in these high stakes situations that her client or patient needs her unwavering support, her warmth, her extensive knowledge, and her patience.

I recommend Dr. Danielle Delaney extremely highly to help anyone to handle any life transitions or difficult situations. She is indeed the best of the best. Mostly, I appreciate that she gave me the one thing that everyone else, myself included, always seems to behave as though they have a shortage of — her own TIME. Danielle truly pays attention fully when it matters the most."

Sincerely,
**Jane Doe (client prefers to remain Anonymous)**

"Danielle is a highly intelligent and intuitive person whom I have known for many years. She has a great work ethic, and laser focus. I have known her as a capable confidante and healer, and I am aware that she is most confidential when handling her clients' matters. I am truly confident that, in her current position as a doctor and as a Crisis & Spiritual Counselor, she will bring both great insight and compassion to her work. She will continue to excel in this work because of her fine abilities and talents to help others in crisis."

**Kim Lentz, Actor: Theater/Film/TV**

"My experience working with Danielle has been nothing less than exceptional. I had the opportunity to work with her when she was assisting a family with their needs. The quality of her work was impeccable, from her clear, detailed communication to her strong work ethic and ability to handle enormous responsibility with ease. My team was also impressed with her, which resulted in our ability to choose her as our first choice for any referrals for additional clients in need of the services she offered. Additionally, she is a first-rate individual whom I'd recommend to anyone desiring quality, confidentiality and professionalism."

## Gary Peskin, Rose's Agency & Rose's Agency Home Care

"A very solid individual with a strong moral compass. I have always found her to be dependable and a great confidant. If you are someone who may require her services, know that you are getting one of the best."

## Jim Michaels, Producer / Director at Warner Bros.

"Danielle Delaney was a true saviour to my daughter and to our family after my daughter was having a difficult time coping with a violation. She did not want to go on with university. She did not want to go on with her life. Danielle was there when we needed her and continued to be there, months after. She is true. She is the real deal.
Thank you Danielle!"

## Charmaine Werth, Client

"I have had the pleasure of knowing Danielle Delaney for over 18 years now. We originally connected through our passion for animal causes. Over the years we have worked together on a multitude of various charities, benefits & productions. I have always had the utmost respect for Danielle's work ethic & unwavering determination. Not only does Danielle have a heart of gold for helping others, she is also highly intelligent, quick-witted, organized, charismatic and is one of the funniest people that I have ever met. There is not a subject in the world to which she isn't able to bring some kind of substantial expertise. She is such a rare human being because when she is working with you, it's like having your own encyclopedia, dictionary & thesaurus all in one! When you combine her compassion, leadership skills, extensive knowledge & her continuous drive to help others —

she is just truly a force of nature, and a force of nature that I am so proud, fortunate & honored to call my friend! "

**Angelica Bridges**

"The definition of a Counselor, according to Webster's, is "one who gives advice and counseling..." a simple, to the point description. But to expand on that, while a person trained to give guidance on personal, social, or psychological issues is a uniquely qualified professional, it still takes a very special individual to rise above the definition and go far beyond what's mandated. Dr. Danielle Delaney is that and much more. I've witnessed her tireless, determined, highly-skilled work as a knowledgeable professional for her clients...and personally...when I myself entered a nightmarish crisis that struck me to my core. She has not only been there to shine a bright and comforting light in a very dark place, but I thank her for being a lifeline to me in navigating my way through the chaos and fear. In addition to the excellent skills, knowledge and experience required in her industry, I've also been fortunate to watch her teach those she counsels in not only getting their lives back, but in maintaining balance and order.
The American scholar William Arthur Ward, offered this about teachers:

"The mediocre teacher tells. The good teacher explains. The superior teacher demonstrates. The great teacher inspires." Dr. Delaney inspires. Inspires and provides the necessary bridge for those in crisis."

**Wanda J. Reese, Medical Writer**
**Bureau Chief, News Reporter/Producer/Anchor, WUWFFM, NPR**
**"Morning Edition" local segments**

"If you have the opportunity to have Dr. Danielle Delaney as your Counselor, or as your advocate in any capacity, and you take that opportunity, you'll find that you have made the best move you could possibly have made. She knows from personal experience how difficult it is to overcome adverse circumstances--ask her to tell you what she has experienced, and you will be transfixed. She is a true inspiration. She certainly inspires me more than anyone else I know. She has helped me through challenges as terrifying as brain tumor surgery and monoplegia, along with the related need to take temporary disability leave from practicing law, and as deeply personal and universal as grieving the death of a beloved family member. She has assisted others experiencing almost unimaginable tragedy, even while recovering from her own. With diamond-sharp intellect and the most gentle, pure kindness anyone could ever have the good fortune to experience, she manages to bring you back to yourself with warmth and a wonderful sense of humor. I am so delighted to be able to say that my little sister, Dr. Danielle Delaney, is truly unparalleled in her field, and that her place in my heart is equally unparalleled."

**Kelly Williams Ching**

*"You can write me down in history
with your bitter twisted lies,
You can trod me in the very dirt,
and still, like dust, I'll rise."*
**Dr. Maya Angelou**

# Chapter 1

## DEMOLITION

Each time that one of those "I Shouldn't Be Alive" or "Lived To Tell" true crime television shows or movies or books pop up, I entirely identify with them.

Now, let me tell you – a statement like this from me or from anyone means that they are a member of a club which none of us ever wanted to join. That is the club of survivors of extreme, horrifying, terror-inducing, life-altering trauma. We understand one another, whereas to others, we may as well be speaking a foreign and unknown language.

The demolition came during what I had thought to be the best time of my life.

In 1968, I was born Danielle Willard Williams. Twenty-eight years later, in June of 1997, I earned and achieved the coveted Screen Actors Guild membership status and acceptance, and was informed that someone in the Union already "had" my name, and that I would have to change mine. I legally changed it to Danielle Leigh Delaney, using names in my family's history, to create my stage name and my legal name, for the rest of my life.

By age 37, I had lived a charmed and extraordinarily good life with only ordinary difficulties, had a great "day job" and was in phenomenal physical shape and excellent health. I was at peace with my life choices thus far, and was enjoying my very storied personal life and my occupation as a working model and actor in the entertainment world of Hollywood, California. On the night that my life changed forever, I was attending the red carpet birthday gala of my closest friend. In the last decade, I had guest-starred on a show, "Arliss" on HBO with the actor Shemar Moore, I had appeared on "FAME: LA" and also had a tiny walk-on part on "Melrose Place." I had co-hosted an episode of "Ripley's Believe it or Not!" and had dated Robert De Niro and other actors that were household names. That, in itself, is truly another book. I was doing print modeling and had graced the covers of international hair catalogs around the world, and appeared in Verizon ads and booked ads for other major products. In a sea of trillions of people who all want the same thing, which is to book paying acting and modeling work and to be noticed and recognized for doing what they love, I was succeeding. People back then and currently, erroneously, have thought and said that I was a Playmate or a Baywatch actress. These errors even ended up in the press. I knew many of both, so it may be a "birds of a feather" sort of mis-understanding and there is nothing wrong with being either, but I am *neither*...I was a standard Print and Commercial model and enjoyed only small acting roles on other series, and was not ever part of the aforementioned. I tell you all of this so that you may clearly see the stark contrast of my prior life with my life after demolition. I was very much enjoying my friends, my work, and my fairly young life. Looking back, I will admit that it was a rather glamorous existence, and I don't lack appreciation for that at all.

I loved every minute of it.

There was no hint, other than an odd sense of foreboding deep inside, that my life would be altered forever by the events of that evening.

Most people can't even relate to the lifestyle of living in the entertainment world. Other than other models or actors who understand what it is to work in that field and play on that playground, people really don't know. There is a seedy side that is shown in movies about the industry, and it is no fantasy. I recently conducted an interview about exactly that on my radio show, "The Real Deal With Danielle Delaney." Please go to www.voiceamerica.com/show/2552/therealdealwithdanielledelaney and www.expectdelaysbook.com or www.danielledelaneycounseling.com to connect with me and with my show topics. I want others to know what to avoid. It's a decadent life where, although you may work and maintain a 9 to 5 job to finance the career that is your passion, you do have to go out to events, network with others in your field, and often reap the benefits of getting a foot in the door by doing so. Here is the truth. Your real friends are few, your acquaintances are many, and nothing is what it seems. To be in attendance at the event of a true friend, one considers oneself lucky. It's a chance to let your hair down, so to speak. Less professional pretense, more genuine enjoyment. This was my mindset that evening as I sped in a cab to Angelica's birthday event where she would also perform on stage, which I deeply love to watch her do, and where I would see many familiar faces who also knew both me and my multi-talented friend. I was, most honestly, having the time of my life.

Admittedly many cocktails, conversations and hours later in a stadium-sized venue, I was ready to go home. I felt woozier than I should have for the amount of alcohol that I had consumed. I wandered outside to find the car and driver that my friend often utilized for crowded red carpet events like this one. As is the norm, there were many similar town cars and limos lined up outside of the venue, but I recognized our car. Or so I thought.

I opened the door and stepped in.

I had opened the door to hell.

What followed is a blur of sounds, smells, tastes, and painful sensations and memories. I was punched in the face repeatedly, blow after blow rattling my brain inside of my skull. I put my hands to my face and they were then covered in blood. I was stunned, never having experienced being struck, ever before in my lifetime. I was hearing awful screaming and wished that it would stop, not knowing that the screams were coming from me. A hand was held over my screaming mouth and my nose.

Other hands wrapped around my throat. It seemed that the hands were coming from everywhere, and they were. I couldn't stop them, and I couldn't breathe. My top was being unlaced, the pretty top that I had so carefully chosen and laced and tied myself. My jeans were torn open, ripped past the zipper; a hand shoved itself inside of them. I lunged for the door handle and was shoved back with mocking laughter. I heard the now forever unforgettable sound of the automatic car doors locking. "Clunk-Clunk." Locking me in. I began to hyperventilate. Out of the corner of my torn and bloody eye, I saw my purse being thrown out of a car window with more laughter from all of the men as the automatic window went up again.

I now had no phone, and no money or identification.

I was slowly being turned into "Jane Doe."

That is what they call unknown bodies in the morgue.

This was a complete demolition of life as I knew it.

I heard more and more laughter. A language that I had heard often but didn't speak or study myself was being spoken very, very rapidly. I recognized it as Farsi, having many Persian friends since childhood, where I grew up very privileged and fortunate in the rolling hills of Los Angeles and Mulholland Drive, in the hills high up above the famed San Fernando Valley. My beaten head was spinning as I looked around the limousine and through the blood in my eyes I quickly counted. One, two, three, four,... five, six, seven, eight. Eight men in the stretch limousine. Eight men, laughing and beating me and holding my limbs down and holding me by my throat and by my ankles, and pulling off my shoes and my clothes.

Eight men, and me.

I was beaten some more, I was raped, I was screaming, and the car kept on driving. I could hear the ground beneath the floor of the car where I lay as I strained through my blinding headache to think. To listen. I remember thinking, *If I can recognize even one word, maybe I can use that information somehow.* I understood nothing but laughter and the smell of sweat and the sickening realization that, wherever they took me, I was not going to be coming back. I understood the words "Chateau Marmont." The name of a well-known hotel. They were planning to go to a second location.

I kicked and I scratched and I kicked some more. All of my efforts were met with laughter from the group, and more and more multiple hands holding me down. I tried to turn myself over and attempted to push myself up with my arms. The small of my back was stomped upon with heavy shoes, and my face fell hard onto the car floor. I felt another body on top of mine, again. I think that's the moment when I left my body. I was somehow observing myself from above myself. There is simply no other way to describe it. I recall thinking, *"So this is what that feels like."* I finally knew what the last moments in the life of a rape, kidnap and murder victim were actually like. I'd read it, I had seen it in movies, but I thought, "Now I know. So this...*this* is how it feels."

I realized that the next logical step after kidnap and rape is murder.

Every morbid movie, every Dateline mystery, all of the things I had watched over the years and had found terrifying but extremely interesting flew at lightning speed through my head. I suddenly recalled the self-defense classes that I had taken. I had worked for a firm called Siegel & Feldstein years ago and, very honorably, they had sent the employees through a weekend self-defense workshop. I remembered two things that were vital: when you are pinned down, move the opposite arm and leg and shift the assailant's body weight. Tuck your chin when you are being choked so that the hand is moved off of your windpipe so that you can breathe. Also, from the movie 'The Silence of the Lambs,' I recalled the advice to make the victim "human" to the captor. I wanted to do everything that I could to keep them from taking my life in order to preserve their own lives and freedom.

I had a split second to shift and to push myself up as one man moved off of my body. With a shaking voice I said "My name is Danielle, and I have a son named Reza. He needs me."

This name means "King" and was a friend's child's name. Sons/men also have more "value" than daughters/women in this culture. I went on, looking down. I said, "I didn't see you. I don't know your faces. I won't tell anyone. Please let me go. Please. Let me go. PLEASE." I begged and I begged, for my life.

I heard the doors unlock and a door open as the car flew down the street. I was forcefully kicked, in my lower back that had been stomped, from the cabin of the car into the street that moved below me. I remember the sting of my skin hitting the ground and tumbling and rolling.

I awakened later from being unconscious in dirt, in a puddle of my own blood. I very slowly sat up and felt pain shooting down my arms and my legs and in my head. My knees cracked as I wobbled and rose to my feet. My head throbbed and I could only see out of one eye. My clothes were barely on, and I struggled to pull the jeans over my hips and to close the top. Everything was covered in blood. I put my hand to my head, and a clump of blood was in my hand. To this day, I have no idea how far I wandered barefoot to find my home. The only thought I can recall is wishing that I had shoes, and wanting to hide. I was afraid that they would circle the roads and come back and find me still alive.

Somehow I made it, as the sun was coming up. I had a "hide-a-key" buried near the 1920's little cottage where I lived. I dug it up, and slid the key into the lock with relief. I walked into my house and looked in my full-length hallway mirror. I screamed.

My head was misshapen. One eyelid was ripped and the eye swollen completely shut, one eyebrow far higher than the other. Blood caked my hair, my nose was twice its normal size as were my lips, and my clothes were covered in blood. Oddly enough, I walked to my small kitchen and opened the freezer to take out a package of frozen peas. My parents had always put a bag of frozen vegetables on any injuries and I wanted to lie down and put it on my head. My head was spinning, and I kept falling down.

I had a landline telephone and it began to ring and ring. I answered it and it was a friend who had been at the event and she said they were looking for me, where had I been? Why wasn't I answering my cell phone?

I told her I had been taken by some men who beat me up and raped me and that I just needed to lie down, my head was throbbing and I wanted to go. She yelled at me to stay awake and she called 911.

It seemed like the ambulance was there in a second. The fire captain asked if the posters in a box on the floor and photos with friends on my mantle were a roommate or sister. I was confused by the question and said "No, that is me." I was unrecognizably beaten. I was placed on stretcher and I remember a flurry of questions, and vital signs being taken. A woman paramedic and firefighter named Sheila was comforting me in the ambulance.

At the hospital, I was questioned by police, put into a machine to have a CT scan on my brain, and I was fighting to get out of the machine, so I am told. I'm sure I had been reliving being held hostage just hours ago and was, and still am, claustrophobic. I remember very little of this process. I have no idea what I may have said but I called my parents, and my father arrived shortly thereafter. A look of complete shock and horror that I have never seen before or since was on his face. His mouth fell open. My eloquent and brilliant father, a world-famous and celebrated Harvard doctor and professor and author and famous jazz musician, founder of multiple world-renowned organizations, lauded public speaker and performer, was startlingly completely speechless.

I recall telling him, "No. No, please go and tell them to help me. I need to do the rape kit, and they are instead giving me Ativan and putting me in a corner to wait for stitches in my eyelids. I am being treated the way that a beaten Black homeless person must end up being treated; I am being *ignored.*" I've never forgotten for a minute what that felt like. I said, "Go and tell them who you are, and that I am your daughter." Neither of us even hugged or cried, both too much in shock to even express emotion.

My father flew into action and did exactly as I said and, as ever, far more. I was taken in for the rape kit, which is much longer than you could ever see in a montage on TV, and far more invasive than I can ever express. You are scraped, prodded and photographed with a flash in the most raw and painful of places. It is an experience that one can never, ever forget.

My father drove me home, silent and thinking, incredibly pensive as I babbled restlessly, nervously. We got out of his shiny new apple-red Mercedes, and a young Black homeless man in my neighborhood named Bryant, to whom I often brought food and clothing, ran up to me, alarmed by my appearance, and was asking me what had happened, and reached to hug me. My father was upset and pulled me away, saying not to talk to strangers. I said "No, that's Bryant and I know him." My father, although always compassionate to others, was not having it, having seen enough for one day and undoubtedly thinking of and having to imagine men violently hurting his youngest daughter for hours, just hours earlier. I will never forget the look on his face, and in his eyes. I had never in 37 years seen my incredibly powerful and fearless father ever look so defeated. He was shattered. He is strong beyond words, and has a more efficient and effective way of compartmentalizing trauma than I have ever seen in my lifetime. He knew that we would survive this, but looked more hurt and devastated than I had ever seen. I can't imagine his thoughts, concerns, anger, and his fears for me as he drove himself home, thinking and alone.

My mother arrived. She, too, looked terrified and horrified, and she held me, and she hugged me tight until it hurt. My strong, beautiful, tenacious, talented, educated, artistic, cultured and worldly, elegant and brilliant mother, who is phased by absolutely nothing, still didn't break down in front of me. She answered my every whimper of pain with a suggestion, or a hand to help me. She stayed on my couch and took care of me. She let in the several friends who visited me.

She asked questions and I answered, and she took diligent notes. In the days that would follow, she would share any information from me with the detectives who stopped by, and with the fire captain that kept coming by to see how I was doing.

I remember my mother taking tweezers and pulling shards of glass from the bottoms of my feet. I remember my mother, upon hearing me say that I scratched and I kicked, scraping under my fingernails for the skin of my attackers and finding a lot of it, placing it in little band-aids that she labeled carefully and placed in baggies, hoping that the police could use more DNA to find the men who had raped and beaten her child nearly to death, and then threw her from a moving vehicle. She heard me howl with pain from my aching back and legs as I attempted to simply get into the bathtub. She looked at my back and told me that there were imprints from shoes on me. My mother told me that I screamed out at night in my sleep while she slept on my couch, and that I would punch and kick in my sheets whenever the medicines finally got me to sleep. I have no idea how she coped with seeing all of that.

This event was a wrecking ball. Life as I knew it was over.

In the aftermath of traumatic events, you have no map; you are on a winding road and are lost, with no sense of direction whatsoever. The shock and the confusion are complete. Nothing up to this point in your life has left you trying to steer in the fog, seeking aimlessly for some sort of normalcy and guidance, quite to this degree. You are entirely off-track in every way, unsure, and shattered. Your belief system has been altered and you no longer know what to believe about life, about people, about trust, and the shock can last for longer than most expect. There is no longer an internal GPS that can guide you; it was shattered by the wrecking ball. You spin; you stall. Each time you try to turn over the engine and you sputter to life, it shuts off again, to your frustration. You feel completely void-of-course, and you are correct in feeling this way...this is entirely unfamiliar territory.

In the days, weeks and months that followed my own kidnap, rape, and attempted murder, my disillusionment with the legal and healthcare system was complete. Detectives interviewed me as though I should have more answers. Red-light cameras yielded no results. The cameras at the party venue were not working that night and caught absolutely nothing, so there were no faces to look at to see if Angelica (who had been the guest of honor at the party) or I recognized anyone. Although I did do the invasive rape kit, the DNA was not tested yet and possibly never was (please go to endthebacklog.org to help to change the laws and procedures nationwide), and my urine showed no trace of the Rohypnol or other drugs that I'd had a feeling may have been slipped into my drink during the event, because it leaves the system too quickly to be detected. I was sick from the "morning after" pill that they give you when you are raped, sore from the shots given to prevent diseases, sore from the rapes and from the beating, injured all over my body and healing from a very serious concussion and worrying about the tests I took to screen for STDs from the rape. I was told that I would need to test for HIV every 3 to 6 months, to make sure that they didn't take my life, after all. My many calls and questions to the police were treated like a nuisance after a while. I could not sleep without nightmares; I could neither eat, nor relax.

I began to drive around at night, looking for clues of where I had possibly been left, looking for a memory or guilty face that I might recognize and I was told to "stop interfering in my case." I argued that it was "*my* case," so that made it *mine* to investigate. My leg injuries gradually got worse and worse, and my father sent me for double leg and knee MRIs, and I had to be drugged in order to stay in the machine.

Additionally, we finally discovered fraud on all of my accounts. These men or someone else had possession of my wallet, which had been the least of our concerns. I now had to deal with identity theft and fraud on top of all of my mental and physical trauma. People began to distance themselves as they could not relate to me, and I was asked to stop showing the photos of my beaten face to people at the financial management office where I had worked, which I was doing because I had overheard one older woman saying that if it had happened to her, she would "be over it by now" and heard a man at work saying "who gets into a car full of men?" as though this were my fault. I wanted to show them what they had not seen, and what they could never feel. I was often falling asleep at my desk since I did not find sleep at night, keeping watch over my own body, as survivors tend to do. I cried in the bathroom stall at work, and could no longer go on castings after work. My injuries, brain trauma and memory loss were extensive, I felt lost and misunderstood, and entirely isolated because I was indeed the only person I knew who had been present through what was done to me. I was simply existing through PTSD, going in circles and in pain, frightened by memory loss of chunks of my history, self-medicating, and on a road to nowhere.

I tell this story of what happened to me to convey to you that I know whereof I speak when I discuss healing from trauma. I know how to work with traumatized individuals as a trained mental healthcare professional, I understand the questions about life and God because I am now a doctor of both Theology and of Divinity, because for years I was studying, doing volunteer work with shelters, churches, and interfaith seminaries, and seeking my own answers, and I know how to help even more instinctively as a survivor of the unthinkable. Follow me, as I guide you in surviving the delay in all areas of your life, and show you the way to reclaiming not only your life, but also your light and your soul, after the demolition of all that you knew and believed to be true.

I am absolutely living, breathing proof that it can be done.

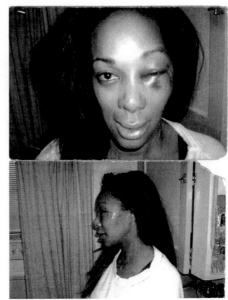

Left: Before.

Right: November 18, 2005. This is the face of rape. This is AFTER I had been given stitches in my face, after the invasive rape kit, and after I had changed my clothes and most of the blood was cleaned off of me. You can imagine how much worse it was hours earlier when I first looked in the mirror and was taken to the hospital in an ambulance. The photo was taken by my father, so that we could document everything for my case. The rest of my body was even worse, with shoe prints and handprints and extensive injuries from both the assault itself and from being thrown from the moving car. I was lucky to be alive. This was after being hospitalized on the worst night of my life.

The following photos have an *intention*. It is not vanity. The intention is to share with you that I was indeed in the prime of my life, and having the *time* of my life when the attempt was made to end it, and they very nearly destroyed it. In those hours, I was robbed of all of this and more. I persevered, and I managed to reclaim it. **The point is that YOU can do so, too.** I am living, breathing proof.

Some photos from my modeling portfolio throughout the years. Photo by Jon Abeyta, who has been my photographer and make up artist since the age of 17.

Photo: Russell Baer. I was only about 23 years old.

One of the international catalogs for which I was the cover model.
Photo by Jon Abeyta.

Early thirties, and still enjoying my acting and modeling career. Photo by Jon Abeyta.

*Dr. Danielle Delaney, Th.D., D.D.*

Photo: Jon Abeyta

Photo: Jon Abeyta

*Dr. Danielle Delaney, Th.D., D.D.*

Photo: Jon Abeyta

Another catalog cover from my modeling scrapbook that I had signed at a fan event for models and actors. Photo: Jon Abeyta

My comp or "zed" card as a print model in the early 2000's. All photos here by Jon Abeyta Photography. Hair by DeLisa Davis.

I was only 17. First modeling job...So young that I had no idea about knock off earrings they had me wearing! Shoot was for Revlon.

A photo session for her lookbook, with makeup artist Julie Brassington. 2004.
Her friend was the photographer.

Photoshoot for makeup artist Julie Brassington's lookbook.

Photo by Lysa Nalin.

*Dr. Danielle Delaney, Th.D., D.D.*

My NoH8 shoot in 2012 with famous photographer Adam Bouska; for this shoot I was billed as "Dr. Danielle Delaney, THE Celebrity Crisis Counselor." Dr. Drew Pinksy, Taye Diggs, Paris Hilton, George Takei, Slash, Khloe Kardashian, Kim Kardashian, Courtney Kardashian, Andy Cohen, Tatyana Ali, Kathy Griffin and millions of other celebrities also did this photo shoot and campaign. It is an anti-bullying campaign against Prop 8. I am PRO LGBT rights as I believe marriage and love are basic Human Rights. I always have and always will strongly support the LGBT Community wherever and however I can by marching and participating in prolific campaigns such as this one.

Celebrities who also did the NOH8 shoot - I was honored to be asked
to participate in such talented company.

**A collection of photographs from over the years:**

Cafe La Boheme, West Hollywood. With friends Kim and Christy,
celebrating my birthday in the early 2000's.

With my longtime friend Bobby Trendy in 2007, at his store.
We had both suffered losses. He had just lost his dear Anna Nicole
Smith that year, and I was still reeling from the assault.

West Hollywood, CA: Nearly a decade later in 2016 with Bobby Trendy
at "Pump" restaurant for dinner, a very favorite place.

With the charming Simon Cowell at an event.

Pane e Vino in West Hollywood, CA. With friends Tin, Christy, and Kim
for my birthday in 2003.

*Dr. Danielle Delaney, Th.D., D.D.*

Beverly Hills, CA in the late '90's. Going out to a benefit with friends.

With Paul Sorvino.

With my late ex, the much loved Dr. Frank H. Ryan. At John Branca's home, 2005.

Izzy Lamas, Lorenzo's beautiful daughter.

I threw Angelica's tropical-themed baby shower. Her firstborn child was due very soon.

A white wedding...the year was 2002.

Hollywood Hills, CA. The late nineties, with my gorgeous and intelligent friend Deanna.

Los Angeles, CA. Painting the town red with Angelica Bridges in early 2004.

These pics were cut and in frames where I lived in the early 2000s.

Beverly Hills, CA. 2015. At Spago for dinner with long-time friend Karen McIntosh.

Beverly Hills, CA. With longtime friend and ex-boyfriend Sean Kanan, back in the early 2000's.

Beverly Hills, CA. With my lovely entertainment attorney and friend, Carin LeVine, at a benefit. 2004.

At peace, in the ocean. Kauai, Hawaii

80 feet down, scuba diving in Kauai, Hawaii.

Scuba Diving in Kauai.

Hawaii, 2013. This was well before the documentary "Blackfish." Now that I've learned, I'd never again be able to stomach swimming with an animal in captivity.

Katana, Beverly Hills, CA. With Romance Supermodel Cindy Guyer and a guest. Early 2000's.

With Ronn Moss, Devin's Hubby and Soap Star.

With the beautiful Jeryl Bryant. Watching my Father's jazz quintet, "Raw Sugar," performing in L.A. in 2006.

My friend from childhood, casting super-agent Johnnie Raines, in Laurel Canyon at his lavish wedding to his wonderful husband Michael in early 2000's.

Las Vegas, 2010. Posing in front of Angelica's poster when she was the Headliner of her show, "Fantasy" in Las Vegas at the Luxor. As you can see, I was excited to support and watch my dear friend sing and perform as the lead.

Hollywood nights with Carrie Gonzales in 2000.

With Angelica Bridges at the "Summer Night Under The Stars" fundraiser for The Brent Shapiro Foundation, for Alcohol and Drug Prevention and Awareness. Voted best drug prevention charity 2016. My makeup artist was Rose Miller.

Malibu, 2010. Andriana with Carrie and Jaxon Stevens and me, at Dr. Frank Ryan's "Bony Pony Ranch" for his charity event and 50th birthday in May, before his untimely death in a car accident just 3 short months later. He was my ex-boyfriend and dear friend for decades, and I was devastated by his death.

Malibu, CA. 2010. With Monique, Carrie, Andriana, and Jaxon at Dr. Frank Ryan's ranch for his charity event for inner city children and his 50th birthday. Step and Repeat.

*Dr. Danielle Delaney, Th.D., D.D.*

Charing Cross Road, Beverly Hills, CA. My lead Nurse and friend, Nurse Christy Adams and Dr. Danielle Delaney, doing Charity Work for The Guardians for Jewish Homes for the Aging. Neither of us ever worked for Playboy; The charity event was just held at the Mansion. Early 2005.

West Hollywood, CA. Dinner With Christy Adams, RN. June 27, 2009 at Sunset Plaza. Michael Jackson and Farrah Fawcett had just passed away on the same day, a couple of days before. Everyone in Hollywood was still in a haze of shock and loss.

Upper East Side NYC 2010 with romance supermodel and owner of 'Guyer's' Restaurant, Cindy Guyer.

Having fun in NYC with fellow model and longtime friend, Cindy Guyer, in early 2000's.

Beverly Hills, CA. I hosted weekly Friday lunches at "The Ivy" on Robertson with various friends for several years straight. I grew up going there as a young child. It's still my favorite. With Angel (Boris) Reed and Catalina Fillipakis in 2004.

Beverly Hills, CA. With Serria Rego at her birthday party, 2004.

With very talented actress, singer and "surrogate daughter" Erica Gluck. 2008. She was then on a TV series called "The Game" and in many shows and films. She's all grown up now. Have known her since she was a tiny tot, and I love her very much.

Erica Gluck, 2008. Growing up!

With the sweet and talented Emmy winner & actress Jennifer Finnegan at a holiday party in the early 2000's. Adore her – she is one of the nicest people that I've ever been so fortunate to know.

With Raymond Aaron, my mentor and publisher!

With mentor Stedman Graham at "The O Factor" conference.

One of my beautiful and brilliant sisters, Kelly Williams Ching, and her handsome husband, Ernest Ching. True Love.

Daddy and GiGi, my amazing, very accomplished and striking Stepmother (Genita Evangelista Johnson) in 2015. I love them dearly.

West Hollywood, CA June 2016. Cavatina at the Sunset Marquis. Taking my Father out to dinner for Father's Day, 2016.

My beautiful beloved Aunt Estelle, Uncle Alfred and Cousin Donna.

My Father, Dr. Richard A. Williams, with Barack Obama. The picture with President Obama was taken before his first inauguration and was on the cover of one of my father's many CDs; this one was titled "A Soulful Jazz Tribute to President Barack Obama"

My gorgeous mother in the 70's, center, stunning in white mink (back then, we didn't know better.) I don't know who the people are to the right or left, but they were family friends.

My father in the seventies. Always handsome, then and now.

Once upon a time. Little Danielle, Age 5, 1973.

Hollywood, CA 2016 In studio, recording. Testing, 123...Countdown to showtime.

One of the 2016 billboards for my radio show on Sunset Boulevard on the Sunset Strip in Hollywood, California! It was a surreal moment to see it looming large and lit up at night.

*Dr. Danielle Delaney, Th.D., D.D.*

Recently, in Hollywood, CA in 2016 happily photographed at my home by Jon Abeyta, while listening to a recording of my own live podcast "The Real Deal With Danielle Delaney" with a fascinating show Guest. On the air, we tell our stories in an effort to bring peace and know-ledge to others around the world, with listeners in over a hundred countries.

# Chapter 2

## BARRIER AHEAD

One of the most difficult things to encounter as a survivor of trauma is the lack of support. Well-meaning friends and relatives say things like, "There MUST be a Victim Advocacy line to call" or "I think that crime survivors are provided for somehow" but usually with absolutely no follow-up or knowledge about the actual process of what comes next. In their defense, if this is the first time that something of such magnitude has happened to someone so close to them, how would they even know what to do? Often they are doing their best as they see it. Even if they do provide resources, at this early stage they are hoping that you'll make those calls, and take the steps needed to help yourself. This is *not* the mental or emotional state in which you find yourself. You find yourself paralyzed and unable to reach out and make some of the choices that need to be made. A support group across town? Great idea, but when you are too tired from night terrors to drive or to get dressed and participate, escaping into the nothingness of a cocktail and some company seems preferable and far, far easier to accomplish. In reality there is nothing that a drink can't make worse, yet newly traumatized individuals are not learning this just quite yet. Some never do.

Natural disasters are a form of extreme trauma. Ask anyone who has survived Hurricane Katrina or Hurricane Matthew, or a terrifying earthquake or fire of great or small magnitude resulting in loss. Crime presents a separate set of emotions on top of the shock, awe and terror because where there are survivors of violent crime and rape, there are perpetrators. What was done *to* you is your own personal Hurricane Katrina, and the storm instead continues and rages on inside of you, including anger at the fact that this was done to you by fellow human beings. Deliberately, and with malice.

When you survive violence at any age, you lose the innocence of the person that you used to be. It is, in effect, a murder. A murder on a soul level, a murder of the person who used to believe that there had to be some good in all people and in all things, that there is a reason for everything. This is one of the greatest barriers that you can encounter – a rape not only of the body, but also of the Soul and of the Spirit. At this point, you don't know it yet, but you are in the battle for and of your life, STILL. You have not survived intact if you cannot ever regain your Spirit and your Soul. They tried to rob you of that, and in the beginning, you may feel as though they have succeeded. Don't you succumb.

**Please do not allow it.**

In my case, I found barrier after barrier to healing. Physical healing had to come first, and as I tried to get "back to normal" and lived in a state of denial that my physical pain was as debilitating as it was, I made matters worse – traveling to see a fairly new, self-medicating friend who lived in a victim mentality herself, having been victimized too many times to count...who wanted to walk around in New York City as was her norm, go out at night and party, and basically behave as though nothing had happened, which we of course wished was the case for both of us. What I did was drink and dance and "feel no pain" and escape from the familiar landscape of Los Angeles and from my case for a week or two. Escapism and ignoring pain and spending time with other suffering souls in denial is not the right idea. Nor was going back to work while still numb, sleepless, fighting Post-Traumatic Stress Disorder day and night, and feeling lost and misunderstood. I was determined to be the same old Danielle who had been systematically destroyed hour by hour inside of that moving cage of a car. That was not possible; and so, I became someone else. Someone who could laugh as her limbs gave out beneath her and she fell repeatedly while out "having fun" with this dancer friend in New York, someone who could just ignore that the injuries to her legs and back were getting worse and not better, someone who could celebrate being alive although she felt dead. Someone who felt afraid of her own shadow and could not sleep, but who was going to go forward and do all of the things she had been doing..."before." I found my thoughts peppered with a "before" and "after" as distinct as the biblical terms B.C. and A.D.

I was living my life after my death.

It was like a fun-house mirror, disjointed and jarring, distorted and confusing.

Conversations that once made sense and felt light or funny left me feeling offended or upset and hurt. I found myself thinking "people just don't understand," and I was correct. Unless or until it happens to them, they do not. Even if a terrifying event happened to them, it wasn't the same exact one. This is an experience that is beyond isolating.

So, you make believe. I certainly did. I made believe that the worst thing that could happen to me had already happened, and I became more of a risk-taker and abandoned thoughts of my own safety. This happens often to survivors, and often survivors are victimized again and again. This was the case for me. Just nineteen months later as I was trying to swerve back into my own lane in life and catch my breath, I was drugged and assaulted, again, while just out having dinner. There was no way to even properly process that something this horrible had happened to me a second time. This is not un-common, and I will get into that and exactly what happened a little bit further down the road.

It's very important to understand that ***being a victim of violence more than once or twice doesn't make it any more your fault than it would be to have been struck twice by lightning. No matter what the circumstance, the predator made a conscious choice to act predatorily and to disregard and to disrespect a human being, period. If you are a multiple-time survivor of violent crime, moles-tation, rape, or any other form of degradation, I really want you to hear me now. It is still not your fault, and it never was.***

In addition to this barricade between the old self and the new self, your entire sense of self is a big question mark now, whereas you used to define yourself as a certain type of personality or as a particular type of person. Everything has been thrown into a tailspin and you can pump the brakes all you like, and still continue to spin. You can't drive the same old familiar course because you need to be taken in for an overhaul, for repairs. You are not that version of You anymore. Yet to know this while you are in the middle of a spin is not the norm. You panic as you lose control, and cannot right yourself.

One of the largest obstacles to healing can be the disconnect with law enforcement or medical personnel, who may mean very well but who unfortunately very often are desensitized and may overlook the need to say, "I'm sorry that this happened to you" as they take down information and data about what happened. The very sad fact is that they hear hundreds of stories similar to yours all the time.

Other people in your life have, too, from television and from movies, and while they may be upset and troubled and want to support you emotionally, they simply don't have the words. They likely have not experienced physical or emotional wounds to this degree in "real life" and honestly do not know *WHAT* to say.

In most cases, even saying "I don't know what to say" would be preferable to the things that DO come out of their mouths. I began to take over my own support group meetings, saying Let's just make a list of the insane and insensitive remarks that people have made, so that maybe it will take the sting out of it for all of us. The therapist leading the group liked my idea, and we did exactly that. I had actually been told "Well, I'm sure that this second time you will get over it much faster" and "Please don't talk about it; I can't relate when you do" by people I had considered friends. One said "I didn't come and see you for months because I just couldn't see your face like that," to which I replied to this charming but self-absorbed soap-opera actor (I knew several, and they are each admittedly rather vain and will each assume that they are the one of whom I speak!) that maybe just once, perhaps it wasn't about him and what HE needed; could he grasp that concept? The very same people who said the "wrong" thing later showed kindness and support and soothed me at times when I needed help, I have to say. I'll give them that. It's just hard to ever forget the insensitive remarks, though, and harder still to move forward with the people who say them. Again, beyond isolating to experience. You lose fleets of people to the feeling of not being "like" them anymore.

In my instance there was fraud and identity theft because my purse was taken, and in other instances of trauma or disaster, it is your entire home, body parts, or presence of mind that is taken by the incident at hand. In each circumstance, different things are lost, whether literal or figurative. You'll definitely find out who cares about you in times of plenty rather than in times of want. It will be surprising, I can promise you that much. Over the years, you will even notice who has any recollection of what you told them. I had friends, even people working in mental healthcare, who had a completely inaccurate account of what exactly had happened to me or at what location, and seemed surprised that it bothered me when they would casually recount the story to someone in front of me, that they had no clue about something so instrumental and so destructive in my life. The limitations of others become clear. It is not a pretty picture and is more isolating each time. I could hardly keep up physically walking with a friend or had nightmares, and was asked if I was a hypochondriac by a friend working in healthcare. I was stunned by the coldness. You are rebuilding your life for years, and people behave as though you have a leisurely existence. Healing from trauma is far from that. It is heroic measures on your part every single day, and being misunderstood and weathering that storm, constantly. No small feat, and others have no idea what that is like. I recently was told by a new male client that a woman that I knew and still called a "close friend" told him that my assault did not happen. That was an insult to my soul. I cannot imagine why anyone would say that, but the hits tend to keep on coming while you are healing. I had another so-called friend that sold a tabloid story about my dating Simon Cowell and who made over 25 grand from selling this information, and the story once printed was only about half true. I figured out who it was that planted it pretty easily. I had never been a person to publicly tell private tales. I was repeatedly hurt by both "friends" and by strangers during the most difficult period of my life. The truth is that people really do have their own limitations, as well as their own twisted motives about which we may know nothing. An example of lack of sensitivity in recent news is the manner in which the Stanford Rapist was referred to firstly as an athlete who made a "mistake," while his very brave victim and survivor suffers immeasurably as she lives with what he did to her. I take every opportunity to correct people with the facts: that "man" is quite simply a rapist who can also swim. Insensitivity abounds.

The emotional wounds may start to heal partially if you have a parent or sibling, or a great therapist and support group for support. You may seemingly take leaps forward in getting outside more, getting back to work, exercising, seeing friends and some semblance of normalcy, yet the stark reality is that it takes very, very little to cause a setback. You are still in foreign territory although you are feeling your way through and trying to strike out in one direction or another. Your trauma response is acute now, and things that may not have rattled you very much before the wrecking ball smashed through your life may now shake you to your core and exacerbate any flashbacks that you are having.

I attended a convention that I had attended years before, an event for models at a large convention center where fans of particular "glamour" models making appearances there could obtain signed photos of them or signed magazines and catalog covers or posters, or take photographs with us. Models such as Dita Von Teese, actresses and "cover girls" from catalogs like myself, and pinup poster models are all in attendance at this event, many of whom I knew from my circle of friends. At the time, I thought it was a move forward to show up and take my place at my table, to talk with people, and to network. Even though my brain injury had caused me to lose memory and had altered my handwriting, which is common with brain injuries, I was looking forward to signing merchandise and to processing the usual "meet and greet" electric energy.

What happened at that event set me back for several months.

I went to the restroom and did what one does in any bathroom stall... sat down on the seat to use the facilities. This was a large bathroom with many stalls and a lounge area and mirror, which was usually full of women primping, but it was empty when I had entered. I couldn't seem to actually relax and "go," because, I figured, I was tense. I sat, I breathed for a minute, and I focused on identifying what emotion I was feeling. With a sense of deep dread, I recognized what it was: *fear*. The hairs on the back of my neck stood up, and I had goosebumps, and I had absolutely no idea why. It occurred to me to lean down and look under the stall beside me. What I then saw was a pair of feet in very large men's shoes in this stall right next to me and adjoining mine by a thin wall. In the women's restroom, where I was otherwise alone. Someone who should definitely not be there was breathing on the other side of this wall.

My heart pounded in my chest and my mind raced. Was I mistaken? Many of the women, being models, were extremely tall...perhaps this was a tall woman with large feet? Maybe she was wearing masculine shoes? Maybe some man was in there, just by accident?

No. *No.* I knew that it wasn't. I knew it, because my Fear was telling me that there was danger close by. It told me before I saw the shoes, and before I tried to process it logically. Energy does not lie. **Fear does not lie.**

I wanted to go and tell a security guard, but knowing that this man in the next stall was watching and waiting for me to emerge from the stall so that he could grab me was reason enough to stay put. I stayed seated, reminding myself all that I could to breathe, and telling myself to just wait. *Wait.*

Wait, until someone else walked into that bathroom and I would not be alone with only "him."

It felt like an eternity, but likely, it was really only a few minutes. I strained to hear the door open, and peeked through the crack in the door that is invariably there in all bathroom stalls everywhere. I finally saw a woman walk in through the entrance door, and stop to look at herself in the mirror. I sat, and I watched her. To my horror and much like a scene from a horror movie and in what seemed to me in slow-motion, she bent from the waist and flipped her long brown hair forward, upside-down, brushing it from the nape of her neck and down, toward the floor. I thought, this man could just walk out and grab her; she would never even see it coming.

I quickly rose and opened the door to my stall and briskly walked toward her, while talking. I was trying desperately to create the illusion of nothing being wrong. I said, "Hi! You're here! Come with me, I want to show you something!" in a cheerful and perky tone of voice. She looked extremely confused since we had never met, and said, "What?" with a lilting English accent, and I persisted, laughing and saying "Come heeere!" and tugged her arm and took her outside of the bathroom, back into the noisy and crowded hallway of the convention center. She shook her arm free angrily, and said, "What are you doing?"

I hurriedly and very seriously said to her, "There's a man hiding in a bathroom stall. We need to tell a security guard. The way you were brushing your hair...he could have come up behind you, and slit your throat." She stared at me in shock with wide eyes, terrified, and covered her open mouth with her hand.

There was simply no time to talk. A security guard brushed by us. I grabbed him. I told him that a man was hiding in the ladies' restroom. He looked at me for a long moment, and I could see that what I had said just did not compute, didn't register. I told him again. He said something into his radio as he strode purposefully toward the bathroom, and he turned and firmly said to me, "Stay right here." I stayed.

The guard came back a few moments later. I asked what had happened. He said,

"You are one very observant young lady." I closed my eyes and shook my head fervently. Again, I asked him with urgency. "What *happened*?" He casually said, "He's gone. I asked him to leave." I parroted what he said to me, incredulously. "You asked him to *leave*? That's *IT*?" and, he nodded, patted my shoulder, and walked away from me.

I was dumbstruck. My thoughts were that this man would do it again, on another floor or this one, maybe this time grabbing someone, raping someone, killing someone's spirit or killing someone. I'd recently seen a news story where a molester grabbed a child in a casino in Vegas, took her into a bathroom stall, raped her and snapped her neck, killing her, and left her there. The complete disgust I felt reading that story flooded my body again, and I felt dizzy and nauseous, realizing that it could happen to anybody, anywhere. There was no safe zone, no safe place to park.

I wanted to leave immediately. I told the event director that I was leaving and why, and I grabbed my things and told my friend Angel who was there what had happened. She was a model and actress who had just married and had her first child, and was still pumping breast milk, which I knew that she would need to do in the bathroom. I told her not to go in there alone and to have it checked before and then guarded while she went in. I told her to tell everybody. She, too, was wide-eyed and shaken. I was very visibly shaken, and shaking. I could not stay in the large auditorium full of booths and talking and people even a second longer, and there was no possible way to warn every woman there, hundreds of us. I left immediately and trembled while I waited for the valet parker to bring my car. I shook as I drove home, ruminating and thinking, again, Why me? What would have happened if my Fear hadn't made itself so strongly present and known? What if I had not listened to it? What if it had been someone else, other than me? Angel had said she would *never* have noticed someone in the next stall. Perhaps her fear wasn't as attuned and hyper-vigilant as mine, having been a recent violent crime survivor. Perhaps being a new mother, her thoughts would have been elsewhere, on her child.

I could not stop thinking of the could-haves and might-haves. My thoughts overlapped and I was in a completely panicked state.

I had to consciously make myself stay within the lines on the freeway for the two-hour drive home to West Hollywood. Emotionally I was crashing, and I didn't want to add a literal crash to my distress and panic. Waves of terror were sweeping over me as if I were right back in that limousine again. I could hear the sounds of the laughter, taste the blood in my mouth, and could hardly concentrate on the drive. Everything was a blur. I don't know how I made it home.

As soon as I walked in the door, I called the man that I had been seeing for some time and to whom I felt close, and I told him quickly what had happened while choking back my tears. His answer was, "Things like that are bound to happen in that environment, Danielle. A fan convention courts that. 'Fans' are fanatics, and participating in a signing event for models like that is going to bring that kind of person there."

He was right. He truly was, which is a shame. But unfortunately, it also wasn't helpful. I needed to hear that it was going to be alright, and that I likely felt triggered by this, and that I was understandably very upset and that the security there should have done something more. I needed someone to understand what was going on inside of me, which was that I was in the deep throes of post-rape crisis panic and a flashback from the moment that I first felt the dread and the *fear* that made me look and see that pair of men's shoes. I had been in a state of panic and shock the entire time, from being seated in that restroom to finally being home and seated on my couch. I hung up the phone and just stared, feeling disconnected from the person to whom I was speaking, and from the world. I stared and I wondered, would anyone *ever* "get" it, just how terrorized I felt. I took an anti-anxiety pill, poured a glass of wine, called my mother and told her all about it, and she calmed me down as much as she could, and I could hear the fear in her voice. I thought about how it isn't logistically possible that even she will be here for me forever in any moment such as this. Even with her unwavering support, to me, I was painfully alone.

I didn't leave the house for days.

This is just one instance of being triggered by something that can take you right back to the moment of impact. With Post-Traumatic Stress Disorder, which I did not yet know that I had, it feels as though the dangerous event is NOW. Rape Trauma Syndrome as well can be debilitating and is an entirely different and cyclical set of emotions and physical responses. Flashing red "DANGER" signs flash in your mind. Indeed, there was definitely danger present again in this instance. Yet there are lesser events that can elicit a similar response for a survivor who has not yet learned and developed strong coping mechanisms for the occurrence of triggers. Someone shouting, someone jumping out at you or opening a door that you didn't expect to open, any startle; a sound, a taste, a smell, any reminder of the event may take you back into the very emotions that you felt during the original traumatic event. You will not know what the triggers are, until you are triggered. As I said, the hits, as they say, keep on coming. You are exhausted by this daily, but are agitated, and cannot relax or rest. *Hold on.*

You have reached the four-way stop sign of PTSD, where no matter what you do, no matter which way you WANT to turn, you cannot move forward alone.

# Chapter 3

## FALLING ROCKS

You are in an avalanche at this point, when triggers are returning you over and over again to your trauma, and you are in desperate need of help. I know that I was.

Experiences that trigger you are like an uphill grade where you will continuously backslide, Sisyphus pushing forever forth upon that burdensome stone. I felt I had lost that internal compass that I had always had, that pointed me to my own Due North. To feel that lost on the road of life is beyond isolating. Even if you do know people who have been through rough situations, perhaps better or worse than yours, it isn't the same experience. You will feel that nobody can truly grasp or understand what you are going through. It's a lonely road. The blind curves ahead for you are likely to be things with which you have no prior experience or tools to handle.

Looking for a Crisis Counselor or another therapist who specializes in trauma is vital right now. Check out my page, www.danielledelaney counseling.com and www.ExpectDelaysBook.com.

Be brave and look for help. It may save your life as you try to steer through the wreckage. A guide will help you to get through so much of the difficulty, so reach for one.

Anger that bubbles inside of you like a 'road rage' every time that you are cut off in your pursuit of getting back to where you "were" is a *huge* red flag. Anger is looked upon by so many as being a bad thing, which is true if there is rageful acting-out and behavior. Depression, however, is anger turned inward on oneself when it is situational, and not clinical or genetic. In the circumstance of surviving life-altering trauma, you can certainly expect to be depressed and angry, railing against God or the heavens and whatever you were raised to believe. How could this have happened to you? **Why?**

It makes sense to have these questions, and I certainly did go through a soul-searching process for years. It isn't something that others not on your journey will understand. They are not *meant* to understand it; it is yours. While going through it, though, it feels gloomy and miserable to be in your skin. Therapists who do not specialize in Rape Trauma Syndrome or PTSD or Special Victims, Crime Survivors, Adults Molested As Children and Rape Crisis may hear your cries of sadness and do what they think is best and prescribe antidepressants and sleep aids. While I don't think this is the wrong thing to do in every case or for a certain duration, I personally prefer a more holistic and spiritual healing approach with my own clients, and when I was going through the darkest of years of healing, I came to the organic realization that

I was SUPPOSED to be depressed. Why *wouldn't* I be? Some emotions need to, and have to, be felt. Losses need to be mourned.

At some point, the question can be raised within you, Why *NOT* me? I don't condone or excuse anything that may have happened to you or that did happen to me, and happened to me more than once. Looking at statistics, however, for how many women are raped in their lifetime, which is one in three, or how may women and men are molested, or how many people endure hardship and loss and natural disasters, and even in the instance of random disasters happening by chance...why not me? Why not you? We are all special and unique, and we also are all just as likely as one another to go through pain and suffering and brutality at some point in our lifetime.

Pain in life does not discriminate. There is not one lane for *me*, and one for you. Class, color, education, country — lightning can strike anywhere at all, and demolish and destroy all in its path. As humans we have a choice of how we are going to handle that which does happen to us. If we give up that choice, hope is lost. I encourage you to have hope. There will be light at the end of the tunnel, and the sun will rise. Meanwhile, the avalanche of pain can continue to fall upon you as you begin to reach for healing. I want you to know that it isn't unusual to stumble. We all stumble. It is up to you to continue to reach for more help and to make that stumble part of your dance.

Dealing with the legalities of a court case, in the rarer instances where a perpetrator is caught, can be daunting. My perpetrators in my own kidnap and rape and attempted murder were never caught. In the second assault case in my life, only 19 months later, where I was drugged at a dinner and raped, which is called Drug-Assisted or Drug-Facilitated Rape, there was an arrest made and it was our word against his. Yes...he raped more than one person, more than me alone this time. Drug-Assisted rapists very often do. I was not drugged alone; this happens to entire groups of people. I will discuss this more in depth further down the road here. Still, whether the District Attorneys can or will prove consent is fraught with more obstacles than even the best television dramas or movies can portray.

Meanwhile, lives are going on and moving forward around you. What they can or cannot prove cannot become your reality. You DO know what happened. ***Absence of evidence is certainly not evidence of absence; it happened to you.*** Evidence being present is also not a slam-dunk, as we are led to believe by fictional stories. The legal system is complicated, and everyone needs help in order to handle it.

When you are in a maze such as the legal system, the wisest thing to do is to look for and research Court Advocates who can help you to navigate the system. Some are free or have sliding scale rates. Ask a family member or a friend to help you, or call Victim Assistance listed near you if it becomes difficult to keep track of resources or follow up with calls. You need all of the help that you can get right now, and the closest helping hand is your own. Visit DanielleDelaney Counseling. com and check out www.ExpectDelaysBook.com for some worksheets, suggestions, and instructional assistance. Keep trying, keep reaching out to different people every day. Other people may not follow through and call you back, which is frustrating and disenchanting. Life has already knocked you down and you are still here, so don't stop trying now. Little by little, you can make progress.

When trauma arrives in the form of a natural disaster, there are losses of property and losses of life to cope with in the aftermath. When trauma is violent crime, bill payment and hospital bills (and/or fraud committed on my accounts in my own case, because they had my belongings) can add insult and an additional feeling of total violation to other grievous injuries both physical and emotional. I had to begin my financial life all over again and was learning to walk again properly in physical therapy with daily frustration while, at the same time, coping with and learning about PTSD and how to manage it and my internal anger. I also had a brain injury and brain trauma from being beaten and thrown from the moving car, and the second assault over a year later made the injuries worse. My body and skull took a beating, being flopped around like a rag doll while being assaulted. I lost a lot of long-term memory and in the beginning, short-term memory, as well. My family was so helpful to me. My younger brother Allen listened to my late night crying calls and offered an ear and support and made me smile. He was busy with his sustainable web hosting company, but made time for me. My sister La Rae, who was busy with her political work, listened to me and also gave me a special deck of cards, with which to play matching and memory games to help work on my memory. My sister Kelly was always swamped at work as a top attorney, as Senior Staff Council for the State of California Office of State Controller, and yet she still took my every crying phone call that I hated my own life. My Uncle Ernest Willard, who worked for decades in mental healthcare, called regularly to see where my head was…I know that I worried my loving family in so many ways while trying to get my life back, so much so that eventually, my mother pleaded with me to please move in with her so that she could know that I was safe. *Rape is the number one cause of homelessness for women. Number one. Let that sink in.* It is hard to handle life on life's terms when you have been violated and people do not understand you. Day terrors are "nightmares" when you are awake; intrusive thoughts. You may begin to self-medicate and drink, or to use other substances, including pills prescribed to you for sleep and anxiety, excessively in order to cope. You shut others out and cannot find your way. This is a slippery slope where many are lost forever.

Even fast food, self-harm in other ways, and a host of other disordered behaviors have their roots in trauma. Many demons that have been put to bed (for me it was eating disorders that I had thought I had long left behind and an affinity for wine) may resurface and rear their heads as you experience Rape Trauma Syndrome. I recall one woman at Group who was eating fast food day and night, and would discuss the lure of the drive-thru window and eating poorly and staying up all night and sleeping all day. All of us watched crime shows incessantly, as they are a reassurance that you are not the only one in the world going through the horror and suffering of the darkness that follows assault. So many behaviors stem from trauma that they are countless. You know them when you feel them steering you into the darkness. It is never too late to turn back, no matter how far down the wrong path you may have gone.

Going to the police station to check on the progress of my cases was always a cause of distress and emotional backsliding for me. Case records are a number, not a person. You feel like a serial number that does not matter. The backlog of rape kits, in particular, is daunting. Please go to ExpectDelaysBook.com to find out what you can do, and to learn about which organizations for whom to sign petitions and participate in fundraisers, in order to help to move forward the process of ending the backlog. I work with foundations that are named on that webpage who help to further this cause, and YOU can help to advocate for all of us. For rape victims, feeling forgotten and discarded is just salt in the wound. You never get your clothes back. Ever. They are now "evidence" which is far more important than your closet, but it's one more surprise.

I went to speak to a detective about my case at one precinct, only to find that my case had been moved to the Sex Crimes Unit, across the city at another precinct. Driving with PTSD is already frightening, with jarring sudden sounds and movements. Driving across town was another few hours of stress to add to the stress disorder. The detective I was told to call had his "DJ party" company name and thumping party music on his outgoing message. I could not believe that this was really happening to me.

I was in a continuous, constant state of shock and panic day after day at the amount of re-routing and re-calculating of my path that kept happening, when all I wanted was a copy of my police report to be sure it was correct or to provide a copy for Victim Assistance or Disability. I was unrelatable to many people I knew, as I would rant about the hardships of trying to navigate the legal system, knowing that the system is simply overwhelmed and that many officers and detectives are doing all they can, yet as a survivor, feeling discarded and disregarded...becoming a number and a box of untested evidence, rather than a human being.

It is nothing like the cases and scenarios on television, where detectives stop by to assist and help you along the way. They may want to help and try to help, but there are too many cases, too many victims, for them to be invested personally in each and every one. Victim Assistance is an organization with the very best of intentions, yet I received a letter from them at one point that "no crime had occurred" that was worded in exactly that way. The letter sent me into a spiral of depression and feeling invalidated in my pain for days. I rallied and wrote a letter back that they need to be far more considerate of the victim in writing such a letter. I did receive nine hundred and thirty dollars, a one-time amount, for protesting their dismissal, and an agent from that office called to say that they only meant that they could not *prove* that a crime had occurred and for me, in the defeated state of mind that I was in, at least that was something. Yet $930 cannot replace or rebuild a life demolished.

I did have a police officer treat me with extra kindness after he noticed my distress as I sat on a hardwood, uncomfortable bench that hurt my injuries and waited to speak to an officer at the West L.A. police station, where I found that my West Hollywood Sheriff's department case had been relocated. I was uneasy because a man was handcuffed to a bench nearby, and making disparaging comments about women and about me, under his breath and within earshot. The officer noticed my tears and apologized that I was forced to hear it, and asked if I needed to sit elsewhere. I remember this, because it was one of the most considerate things that a stranger did for me during this time period. You walk through life with heightened emotions yet feeling mostly overlooked and unheard when others do not recognize your trauma as being as all-encompassing as it is.

Certain situations are highlighted in your mind when you are traumatized. As I was so upset by the comments I mentioned before that were made where I worked, the valet parkers at the Beverly Hills office building where people were insensitive where I worked had a toy drive and the valets noticed that I was touching a stuffed rabbit that looked like the 'Velveteen Rabbit' every time that I passed them and the collection box. They told me that I could keep it and I cried, and one of them hugged me. They had no idea what had happened to me, yet they showed empathy and kindness. I slept with that stuffed rabbit every night although it became tattered. I was sleeping with a stuffed bunny and I was thirty-eight years old. This is an example of how trauma regresses your thought patterns, and your brain. I needed a security blanket or symbol of safety, and it didn't matter how old I was. The smallest things will make a difference at this point when you are traveling through the tunnels of traumatic stress as well as traumatic *growth*.

Your constant Passenger, if you will, is now your extreme traumatic experience and the shadow of it that follows you. How you incorporate this shadow and Passenger into your drive on this road, and whether he obstructs your view of your path temporarily or forever is up to you. Please do visit ExpectDelaysBook.com for a worksheet and some suggestions for coping with this situation as you go through your motions and stages of reaching for help.

You are on an emotional rollercoaster and there is so much work to do to lay the foundation for reclaiming your life. It won't be the same, but it is worth it to recover. As the old saying goes, when you're going through hell...keep going.

# Chapter 4

## YIELD

It is time to slow down and take the time to heal.

For me, getting used to what had happened to me meant getting sick every single weekend, for some period of time. I would crouch in the bathroom, sick to my stomach on Friday and Saturday nights, because somehow my mind differentiated weekdays from weekends, which I perceived as "party time" and I just knew that these rapists, having not been caught, were very likely at it again. Why wouldn't they be? Why wouldn't they be repeating what they had done to me since it had no adverse consequence for them and they were all walking around free? Why not attempt to overpower and destroy another woman, man or child again? I was certain that it was very likely they were doing so, and that thought and imagining it made me physically ill.

Vigilante fantasies are very normal during this period when you are learning to accept that what happened to you. You want to get even. You want to find them and get back at them. My PTSD specialist/psychiatrist told me NOT to go and see "The Brave One" film, starring Jodie Foster. I had seen the movie preview on television, and told him how excited I was to see it. He told me in no uncertain terms not to see it. I left his office after therapy in Santa Monica, drove directly to Westwood Village to a big movie theater to see it and sat alone in the center of the theater. I have always loved Jodie Foster's body of work, and because she had also been in "The Accused" and "Silence of the Lambs" where a woman is held captive, I was intensely identifying with her character in this movie even more than usual. My vigilante fantasies were not just alive and well, they were consuming me and I will admit that I enjoyed them. The very idea that these evil people who hurt me might somehow have to pay for what they had done was a soothing one for me. This, as I said, is normal in this stage. Later, the movie "Taken" had me similarly enthralled. The thought of the captors who "took" me having to suffer was a romantic one for me to entertain.

I didn't want to remain in the tribe of people who can't move forward from the past, who are stuck in some kind of a time warp where someone else's actions defined them. This is when I realized that a spiritual approach was needed.

A spiritual approach is never rushed. This sounds counterproductive when you first hear it, so stay with me. The reason is that events and things that you will learn now are unfolding quickly, but if you are also rushing, you will miss the lessons. Change is happening, and you need to be paying attention to it. Healing takes time. No doubt about it. I can promise you that it will take longer than both you or I would like. When you take your time, the healing is real. Again, it is going to take a lot of your time. You need to yield to and acknowledge that fact and embrace it.

Trying to rush is a natural mistake and a good effort, but close doesn't count. You are going to have to be patient with yourself and you'll need to do the work. I am someone who tends to want results yesterday. I understand, and I'm here to explain from experience the reasons why it doesn't work that way.

Trauma is cumulative. This wrecking ball of an event in your life has taken on a life of its own, and other things that were previously not traumatic may now have a different significance for you. You life has entirely changed because your view of life and your perspective has changed, and it would not make sense if it didn't and had not changed. If you had earlier traumas in your life, they may have their own superpowers right now. Your trauma has trauma, and you are not catastrophizing or making it up – you are a raw nerve, and everything feels like and is an open wound at this point.

I believe that in life there are unwritten contracts and trade-offs. If you gain one thing too quickly, you can lose something else...health, wealth, love, work, the list goes on. When you take your time to reach for what you need, it is more likely to be lasting, and your mental health is not something with which to take chances. Look around you or test this theory and you will see. Nobody has everything all at once, and if you think that they do, it is fleeting or it is not the truth. Everyone has some area of life that they can improve upon. For some, it is sensitivity, and they will not understand or show the amount of empathy that you require to heal at this time. When you are the walking wounded, it is painful to be around other people. It may be easier to be around other wounded people but you can't stay there too long, either, or you risk taking it all on as your own. You may seek your own level right now and find it hard to connect with people who are not also suffering. Vibrating higher and surrounding yourself with others who are trying to heal when you can, in workshops or support groups, can be very helpful right now. It isn't exactly a hotbed of mental wellness, however, so be mindful that you are trying to heal but you don't need to foster a false closeness or form a trauma bond with everyone else in group therapy, although a sense of community is helpful. It has its limits, and there is no substitute for one-on-one cognitive behavioral talk therapy, for Spiritual Counseling and for learning on your own, reading, audiobooks, and taking in different modalities of healing.

The therapist that I saw when my parents were going through a divorce in my 20's was very good and calming, but was not someone who specialized in Rape Crisis. I was urged to go back to work at a time when I think that some other options with my family and social services needed to be explored for my long-term well-being. I felt like I needed to see someone else who had a history of working with trauma. After many distraught phone calls with my sisters Kelly and La Rae and my brother Allen, each of whom always listened to me, as well as my parents and a trusted close friend or two, my longtime friend Juliana finally hit the nail on the head when she did not know what to say anymore, and said "You need to find a support group." Truer words had never been spoken. It took repeated efforts and calls to find one but I did this, and I'll tell you about it. Meanwhile, I was also in treatment with a PTSD specialist once a week, and I believe that the things I learned while in treatment with him helped me to save my own life yet again. It is information that I pay forward to my own clients and they have told me that therapy with me has helped them to save themselves. That means everything to me.

If you had a flat tire, who would you go to? A restaurant? No. You would go to a garage or to someone who had changed a tire before. You want someone who can help you to do what they do on a racetrack in the pit maneuver. You want real and knowledgeable assistance. Do ask every question you'd like to ask about the practitioner's history. They may or may not answer plainly, but what you are looking for is someone who really knows this territory. Reading and studying about something is a strength and is very helpful, but nothing is a substitute for personal life experience. Proceed with caution. You do want help, and you want very experienced help. Support groups and a great Counselor are your roadside assistance on this path. Look for, and, most importantly, ACCEPT help. Look to www.ExpectDelaysBook.com to join my mailing list and to find suggestions and to find out what I am up to and working on, and also visit www.DanielleDelaneyCounseling.com to get in touch with me. Yield to the powerfulness of this experience and trauma that you have been though and survived. Accept it that you have stalled on the road because of overwhelmingly treacherous conditions. When we accept that we honestly don't know best and open our minds and hearts and souls to the wisdom of another to guide us, that is when real healing can begin. There are still many perils on this path; you are going to need to accept your situation as you reach for resolution, and accept some of the hardship to come, knowing that you have support though some of the difficult roadblocks ahead in your healing journey. You aren't quite safe just yet. Hold on. This is indeed the ride of your life.

# Chapter 5

## TOW AWAY ZONE

You will encounter many dangers zones, even as you continue to head toward the light of healing.

The support group that I attended was excellent, and I was proud of myself and of all of us just for getting there every Wednesday night. The drawbacks were few and the benefits were many.

The group leaders were excellent and were volunteers, getting their necessary hours for their studies, and who were, no doubt, as passionate as I am about helping others and learning about them. However, because it was a volunteer organization and a free service, the location was fairly sketchy...downtown Los Angeles near the

Staples Center and at night. A few of the things you can encounter in that area are team mascots in costume where you cannot see their faces, and a very sketchy, dodgy area and high crime. Just arriving, parking, and leaving in the darkness were frightening for already edgy rape victims/survivors.

We all discussed the questions that people asked that made us feel further isolated. Was a woman attacked at her storage unit dressed suggestively? Was a teen at a slumber party drinking or dancing suggestively? Of course the truth was that it did not matter! It helped to discuss WHY such questions were asked. I can tell you, it isn't intended to be cruel. People who haven't been through it want to make sense of the nonsensical, find logic in what they cannot understand, and distance themselves from the possibility by saying internally to themselves, "Well, I don't go there/do that/drink/ dance/go out at night." It doesn't soothe anyone to know that there isn't a specific 'crime and rape hour' and it's disconcerting for others who haven't been visited by a predator in their life to know that they CAN be. It makes sense that they are trying to MAKE sense of it. They can't.

A sign I liked at a police station, author unknown, says "Think You Can't Be Raped? A Rapist Doesn't Care What You Think." Sums it up perfectly. The clear and sad reality.

Author Dr. Anna C. Salter states it very well in her book "Predators: Pedophiles, Rapists and Other Sex Offenders" when she writes: "Oddly then, in our search for meaning, we often assign victims too much blame for their assaults, and offenders too little. Our inconsistencies do not seem to trouble us, but they are truly puzzling. After all, if the offender is not to blame for his behavior, why would the victim be, no matter what she did or didn't do? Our views make sense, however, if you think that we are trying to reassure ourselves that we are not helpless and, that, in any case, no one is out to get us."

Meanwhile, we really didn't need to walk to our cars more freaked out at night, downtown, than we already were.

I ended up suggesting — well, insisting — that we walk two at a time to our cars and that one person drive the other to her car — street parking only, and the streets were indeed frightening at night. This almost discouraged me from coming back after the first time, but I felt such a sense of community being around other survivors that I pushed myself to come back every week and to just find a way to make it work. I committed and made healing my full-time job and if you are able to do so, that is what it takes.

One woman in my support group had been attacked in a supermarket parking lot in the high-end neighborhood of Brentwood, California in the broad daylight. A man forced her into the SUV that she had been driving as she was loading groceries into the car by holding a knife to her back. He then raped her, attempted to kidnap her and threw her from the moving car. She had injuries much like mine and, at times, I found her to be a kindred spirit. They caught her rapist ten years later, and I was her Court Advocate in the courtroom. It was a full-circle moment and it gave me satisfaction to see her attacker in shackles and a prison jumpsuit since I had grown to deeply care about her as a friend over the years since Group. She had suffered immeasurably since her assault and had been hospitalized for emotional issues more than once because of it, as well as having physical disabilities from it, injuries much like my own. However, I did not agree with other things she did, forgiving her rapist publicly in court and, also, asking me how I got so far in my field in many questions, as though my education hadn't been arduous and quite serious since my college years. I felt close, and then distant. The relationships you make in Group may serve you at some points, and hinder you at others. Only you will know. The similarity you feel will also be a painful surprise when it does not stay consistent. We are all so different with our histories and cases, and while we have a trauma bond, we also are individuals. I have a lot of love now for everyone in that group. I wonder where some ended up, and I know it cannot all be good.

In Group, as we all came to call support group, there were jealousies and issues that were not long-lasting but notable just the same. I carried pictures of my assault always, because I found that people often needed a 'visual aid' to understand exactly what I had been through. Not just that my legs hurt, but that they were very injured by being bounced like a ball down the street. I often told people to visualize throwing a ball out of a car going 45. It bounces, skids, flies into gutters and sidewalks and other objects. This is what happened to my body. In order to explain what they did to my face or body, I would show the photos. I didn't know at the time about secondary trauma and how hard it was for some to see. I remember a friend once turning away and saying "No, I don't like to see pictures of my friends beat up." To which I replied, "Well, I didn't enjoy it at the time, and I need you to understand," and our friendship became distant. I showed my pictures at Group, and the following week one of the women said that she really had issues with it. Her issue, which she said she shared with her therapist, was that she now felt "not raped enough" because she "only" had rope burns on her wrists — no need for physical therapy, no stomped on spine, no brain trauma, no stitches in her eyelid and beaten face.

Of course I felt terrible about her manner of processing what I had shown them. This woman had been raped in her own apartment, the light bulbs outside of it having been unscrewed as her attacker lurked in darkness and followed her in and tied her up and raped her in her own home. I assured her that her rape is no less of a rape than mine, as did the rest of the group and the group leaders. I admitted that I was a bit "jealous" of the other girl in group who had been raped in her car at the market, because while I was losing my apartment and unable to work and running out of funds rapidly, she had Worker's Compensation because she was on the job as a personal assistant when she made that supermarket run. However, she had lost her mother, and mine was my very lifeline. The rapes themselves were all horrible; everyone's story varied but the common denominator that bound us together was rape.

This is a good story to keep in mind as you proceed on your journey of self-care and therapy. We are all equal here.

That day in court, as I advocated for my friend and fellow group member ten years later, I was feeling satisfaction for her, and also sadness for myself. Her assailant was sitting there, gray and old now, and would be in jail. Mine were not, not any of them. Yet I had to think and wonder as I helped her though the difficult process of taking the stand as a witness and discussing her case with detectives, how would I handle it if I did have to face my multiple rapists in the courtroom? I would never know.

There are so many Tow-Away Zones in your healing path and there isn't anything you can do to avoid encountering them. Just don't stop there. My Uncle, Ernest Willard, had a long and storied and very successful career as an LICSW from the prestigious Simmons School of Social Work. In providing therapy to his clients, which now included me, he would often say in his clever and inimitable charming way, "Hey — now, stay out of your own head, it can be a very bad neighborhood." He was and is right, and I often say this to my own clients today. Do not stop here. Let go or be dragged...and you don't want to go where some of the darkness and obstacles will lead you. Shift gears and keep on moving. There may be danger ahead but if you rely on one who has traveled this path and knows the lay of the land, you will be better off. Lean on your Counselor and support group. Assess the conditions ahead every day and continue to proceed with caution. You may be on Self-Pity Road, which can be a very circular drive. Keep circling back to therapy.

You do not want to stay stuck or park your future and your life in a Tow-Away Zone. I'll now examine some of the conditions coming at you quickly, flying by in your side view as well as rear view mirrors. What now?

## Chapter 6

## DANGEROUS CURVES AHEAD: CAUTION!

The going is tough, but you must keep moving. If you weren't tough, you would not still be here. As my father has always said to me...You can do this.

Another thing that my dad taught me when he taught me to drive was to WATCH the WHEELS of others. That is how you know their intention ...are they going to pull away from the curb and hit you with their vehicle, or are they pulling in and parking? Are they making a right turn, or about to swerve directly into you, and into your lane? This was a huge lesson, and it serves me still in life today, 32 years after those driving lessons. I am always, always, forever watching the "wheels" of others in life, so that I may know their intentions and what they might do next, and not be rudely surprised by rash or sudden moves.

Some of the dangers in coping with trauma are ahead. Sleeping too much, or not enough or at all, can become a problem. Insomnia may rear its head. The lights are on but nobody is home. The guardrails that you counted on are no longer there. They are nowhere to be found and you are still in a blind tailspin. You need to drive with both eyes open, high beams on, which you do in order to watch for the flashbacks and monsters in your memories, lurking around the dark curves that have become your day to day life of going forth into the unknown. It is very natural to be jumpy and hyper-vigilant. Yet, you also need to sometimes be a body at rest, so that you can recharge. Easier said than done.

Do all that you can to not neglect your "machine" and disregard the basic needs of your body. Make meals on a Sunday and keep healthy meals and snacks for the week within arms' reach. Eating fast food is like giving yourself cheap petrol. Don't neglect do see that you need real body work and repair. What happened to you is a big deal, and it takes its toll in all ways on all systems in your body.

Eating well, even several small healthy portions a day, will get you on the track to craving less garbage and comfort food. You are doing yourself a disservice to eat poorly, and the only one to pay for this is YOU. Again, your closest helping hand is your own. Don't put trash into your body and then expect to feel well. This is within your control, so take the wheel.

Meditation can help you, hypnotherapy can help you. There are meditation apps on Smartphones, and I am in the process of creating an App to go with this book as part of a trauma healing program. I make some suggestions for meditation and healing at www.Expect DelaysBook.com. Please visit the site to join my mailing list so that I can keep you up to date on new modalities as I learn more about them, and guide you toward resources. Some cities have meditation fellowships that you can seek out and attend or other relaxation classes. Some are low cost or no cost. Look for these things, so that you are repairing your engine in all ways in order to prepare for the treacherous roads and paths ahead in the aftermath of trauma.

I recall nights and nights of being awake. We often fear sleep, knowing that the dreams will come which are, more often than not, nightmares. We also have a subconscious way of watching over our bodies at night when trauma occurred at nighttime and even when it occurred during the day. Darkness can be daunting, and everyone else is asleep. It's scary and lonesome, and we don't want to let down our guard. I did this for many, many nights and I appeased myself by thinking that sleeping at any time was good enough. Better that than no sleep at all, but we are naturally built and created to blossom in the daylight and power down for rest at nightfall. It is not easy to reset our circadian rhythms, and I am a self-professed night owl and my entire immediate family are night owls, as well. It is not at all unusual for us to be on the phone with one another at odd hours of the night, and I receive emails from my very busy father at wee hours and he is not surprised when I reply back immediately. However, it isn't as healthful to sleep by day as it is to sleep at night. Hot baths or decaf tea in the evenings, establishing a ritual, and not watching or reading upsetting material after a certain time of day or night can contribute to feeling more relaxed. You can set up phone sessions for counseling in the early evening, so that by nighttime you are spent from expressing your emotions. If you are a night person this can help to reset your rhythm, and waking with the rest of the world to accomplish your plans and goals will make you feel less isolated. It takes time, but it is worthwhile to work on your hours and getting the sleep that you need at nighttime. Aim for 7 hours or more of nighttime sleep while you are fighting demons in your mind and in reality. The legal process, the logistical difficulties in rebuilding your life, and overcoming physical and Soul and Spirit injuries are exhausting in and of themselves. Do everything that you can to get the rest and repair that you sorely need.

Swimming has been something that has soothed me since I was very young. My swimming and my piano lessons from 4 years old onward have always served me well. I find nothing so peaceful as being underwater. As a PADI certified scuba diver, my favorite place on the planet is eighty feet under the ocean. I wanted to swim at the Belmont Shore Olympic Pool to facilitate healing for my legs and my back. I was incredibly self-conscious, because I could not possibly exercise at the athletic level that I had been accustomed to before the assaults had injured me terribly. I felt out of shape and, being hyper-vigilant and having PTSD, I felt watched. There were lifeguards there who observed all of the swimmers and who were probably not paying any particular attention to me at all. Yet, I felt uncomfortable and asked a young lifeguard if there was any time of day that there would not be anyone watching. Empathetic, she somehow recognized me as a trauma survivor. With warm eyes, she said, "It takes time to get through really hard times and hard things that have happened." This wise young woman could tell that I was struggling with being in public at the pool. Her kindness bolstered me, and I thought about Demi Moore in "G.I. Jane" and all of the stories I had read about Madonna overcoming adverse times in her life. I thought to myself, nothing would stop *them*...I need to be like *that*. Emboldened by thinking of these strong women that I idolized, and calmed by the young lifeguard's words, I took to the peace of the water every night, and began to swim again and to heal some of my injuries. I never again saw that girl who worked at the pool, but she made a difference in my life by being understanding. She uplifted my spirit. Never underestimate the effect that your understanding or kindness may have on another person.

Even before the wrecking ball hit you, you may have had an unserviced engine under the hood — you may have looked just fine on the surface but may have indeed been spiritually bankrupt. You didn't even know that you needed a tune-up and may not have ever had a drive toward a Higher Power. That drive will serve you now. You need a jump start to your Spirit. This isn't to suggest that you must follow organized religion unless that is the direction that you lean, anyway. As a Doctor of Theology and of Divinity, the study of God and the Divine, I can tell you with authority that God as YOU understand that concept, a Higher Power, a power greater than yourself, is perfectly enough. Spirituality is not necessarily religious and religion is not necessarily spiritual. Perhaps look for a Self-Realization Fellowship, a spiritual bookstore, or Google search and order or read some spiritual material online. You might have never exercised any connection to a higher power or to anything greater than yourself. Feeling less alone on the planet is soothing to the soul. Giving it a try cannot hurt you and will so much more likely help you. Spiritual Counseling and guidance does not have to be rigid or overbearing or call into question your own beliefs, if you have any. Give it a spin and see how it feels.

Going out in Nature, although it may seem like the last thing you feel like doing, can reawaken your soul. Love, power, truth and light are in the mountains and the oceans. Playing with animals and pets, looking at wild animals and watching birds, feeling leaves crunch under your feet and the wind blow through the trees is healing. Push yourself, and get outside. If a friend can join you that's great, but some of our greatest moments of understanding ourselves are found alone. Drive or take transportation to a safe area of nature and explore. You'll be surprised at how much better you will feel.

I was angry at any God or being that would allow me to suffer so, and allow the perpetrators to go free. I had friends or family or acquaintances who would say things about going to church or temple or a Buddhist meeting or that these men would face their own karma and may be suffering from their own actions, or to pray for them or, alarmingly, that I must forgive them. I had a great deal of trouble with that concept. As an Interfaith Spiritual Counselor as well as a violent crime survivor, I cannot in good conscience pressure anyone to do what I do not find palatable or amenable, myself. I am not prescient. I spent time training in Seminary, yet I have no absolute understanding of what comes in the future. I call this need coming from others regarding wanting to hear you forgive your assailants The Forgiveness Fallacy.

While you are in this unchartered and unfamiliar territory, I believe that one of the most damaging things to your sense of self and your sense of "oneness" on this planet is anyone, anyone at ALL, insisting that your healing begins with your forgiveness of the perpetrators. I think this began with one religion or one self-help "guru" driving home the point of forgiving others to move our own lives forward. I beg to differ. In fact, I won't beg — I insist — on a broader understanding of what this means to us as victims of a crime such as Rape or Molestation or of random violent crime. This means that wait, hold on a minute...my healing is contingent upon ANYTHING having to do with these inhumane perpetrators? *Why?*

Well. It doesn't. You don't HAVE to forgive anyone. You heard it here first. **You simply don't have to do it! Nothing in your life or your future depends upon how you feel about what happened and what was done TO you.** You CAN have your anger and you can allow it to stoke the fires of ambition under you. I used it to tell myself over and over, day in and day out, that I was bent but not broken and that I would fight as I had fought for my life, and that I would not let them "win" and gain my Spirit and Soul and my very LIFE as they had tried to take them from me. As long as it isn't anger turned inward on yourself and manifesting and presenting as depression, who is any religious leader, TV personality, therapist, guru, or author to tell *you* who you have to forgive? What worked for him or her may not be what works for you. I find it to be an unconscionable expectation. Also, why tie your healing to anything outside of yourself and least of all to your attackers? I strongly disagree with that modality and theory. If you want to be forgiving and it soothes your Soul, please have at it, and do not let anything that I say or write dissuade you; that is not ever my intention. I only invite you to think for yourself. I did, and I benefit from it greatly.

*Expect Delays*

Prepare yourself in all of these ways that I have mentioned here, because there is more to be wary about on the trail ahead, and you will need your sharp wits about you more than ever.

# Chapter 7

## SLIPPERY WHEN WET

A slick surface is a dangerous surface on any path. It doesn't matter if you are walking, running, limping or crawling along. A wet road is an unpredictable one. The most unpredictable road that someone going through healing from an unprecedented and unpredictable trauma can take is the road of alcohol and intoxication.

I have been on this road and walked it from one end to the other, so I do know whereof I speak. I was certainly no angel before the wrecking ball hit; I was known to enjoy a good time and if there was a party, I was there with bells on. I started partying early in my life, while going to Bel Air Church camp and bible studies as a teen. Liquor, clove cigarettes, and even pills were around every corner with very wealthy kids. Addiction and drug and alcohol use do not discriminate. Where there are family system issues, there are kids seeking a way to feel better and "take the edge off." I found this to be true in church, in junior high and high school and onward. My family was never any the wiser, because I was a good little liar and cover-up artist as most of us that want to carry on partying have learned to be. I was not an alcoholic growing up, but as a twenty-something and as a young woman in my thirties, I didn't meet many cocktails that I didn't like and want to get to know better. With lowered inhibitions come poor judgement calls, and waking up with a hangover and what I used to call "The Uh-Oh's." Uh-oh, who did I call, who did I run into at the restaurant, to whom did I say the wrong thing, to whom do I owe an apology? It didn't really matter...in the "fancy" circles in which I was running by my young thirties, nobody remembered enough to apologize for anything. We were blissfully unaware, and blissfully ignorant.

I was drunk when the assault happened; I was still drinking when the second assault happened nineteen months later. I still know for certain that something was slipped into my drink both times, which is increasingly common these days and was absolutely common at the time. My drinking had little to do with my awareness of my safety. I took a cab to the party, and I had planned to be safe getting home with my friends' car and driver or a cab if I left early. In the second instance, I used the "buddy system" and was out with a friend who also drank moderately that night and never left me alone. She was drugged and raped, too. I drank responsibly and everything that happened to me still happened. I do not blame the assaults and attacks on any substance. I blame them on the choices made by the rapists. I could say "my" rapists, but I refuse to call these beings mine.

No matter what you were doing, drinking, wearing, or saying, it is not your fault. I repeat. It is never your fault. It is the CHOICE of the perpetrator to take away yours.

Later, self-medicating became an easy crutch. First of all, it was already my familiar friend from my life "before," having a "nice glass of wine" which became three or four, after a trying day or a difficult audition. Social events had centered around being sauced and socializing with other drinkers, smokers of whatever, consumers of what-have-you. I was youngish, and this was Hollywood. I didn't really think twice about it.

As I was healing or attempting to heal, it became an attractive idea to have a drink or several in the city, getting out of my mother's house. I would then need to stay overnight at a friend's house, since the drive at night was too much anyway, and since I did not drink and drive, having lost my dear friend Sharon Barnett, my dear friend Robyn's irreplaceable beautiful sibling, to a drunk driver as a teen.

That was the one and pretty much only thing that I would never do. Everything else, I'd give it a shot. Who knows... maybe it would make me feel better and it definitely made me feel like I fit in more easily and forget my troubles for a while. Now I look back and wonder, who wants to fit into *THAT* scene? Everyone was deadening themselves. However, way back then, I felt the need to blend in rather than to stand out.

***Friends who are drinking are unpredictable, as am I, and as are you. It is the nature of chemicals to alter our brains. It cannot go smoothly.***

I recall one close friend who is bigger than I am lunging across a couch and sticking her tongue in my ear after a few cocktails. I didn't see her for a while. Anything that I don't invite scares me, and it should. I had done nothing to invite an overture like that, and my ears are sensitive and I particularly dislike that wet ear feeling, it gives me shivers up my spine. That was the last thing that I needed. Male or female, any uninvited touch was not welcome and made me feel unsafe. That was not her intention, but alcohol can cause people to be unpredictable.

Other friends courted drama and arguments amongst themselves and then needed me to mediate, which I was in no state to do. Others would pick a fight with me. Once, I got sick on a male friend's rug and he asked me to leave, although I had nowhere to go. He clearly didn't care, and he was another poor decision. Anything could have happened to me. I woke up in my car, which thankfully I did not ever drive drunk, but anything can happen to a person sleeping in their car. The amount of unsafe situations I put myself in after others had caused me so much pain is staggering. **I was counting on altered individuals to have my best interest at heart.** Bad idea.

I realized that separating from harmful behaviors and being mindful of my PTSD was what would be best for me now. I kept more to myself. One of my neighbors and friends was Jennifer Carpenter, the actress who had been in "The Exorcism of Emily Rose" and was just beginning to star on the hit HBO TV show "Dexter." She was lovely and sweet, and I remember the day she booked the part of "Deb," Dexter's sister, when they first cast the show. As she progressed on the show and it gained critical acclaim and success, Jennifer asked me to spend some time with her explaining to her and showing her what it was like to suffer from PTSD, and to teach her what the flashbacks were like. I showed her that I could not have my ankles held to do sit-ups with a trainer – it reminded me of when they held my ankles and took away my shoes when I was kicking.

I didn't know why she needed this information at the time, but it sure made perfect sense years later when I watched the series. She is a tremendously talented actress and was a solid friend, and I was pleased to serve as a consultant to her for her character's experience on "Dexter." She played the part of Deb Morgan the trauma survivor to Emmy-Award nominated perfection. I realized that just maybe, I needed to continue to use my time showing others what I had learned. I felt great doing it.

Finally, having attended a Speak Out event that my mother cut out of the local paper and left on her kitchen table for me to discover and decide for myself whether I wanted to go or not, I began to embark on courses to add to my former Psych studies and degree, and to work with Sex Crime Victims. I had gotten on stage to speak at the event, and after being commended for my speaking, I enrolled in the courses given by the academy that had put on the event.

The classes and internship were arduous ten hour days, and I needed all of my focus to show up every day while I was still in the stages of healing. You cannot miss even one day or be one minute late when training to work with crime victims, trauma and Crisis Intervention or you are automatically disqualified. In school they actually tell you that if your car breaks down, you had better have a bicycle in the trunk. *That* is the dedication that it takes to be fully present as a first responder. Alcohol could not be a part of my evenings if I was to show up at a hospital in the morning and work with rape victims and forensic nurses, and I could not work the rape and suicide hotlines at night with a drink in my system, either. Drinking makes us sloppy, and sloppiness when dealing with suicidal victims' care can result in loss of life. So, I stopped. I had a rough day a few years later when I learned that Social Security Disability wanted back most of the money they had put forth for me. You see, although some friends or others perceived me to be someone from a family that was supporting me, even though I moved home after a few years to live with my mother to heal, I was forced out of necessity to be on Public Assistance during my healing because I could not contribute and take care of myself with my PTSD and injuries. Then, after three years of struggle and trying, I received Disability for my injuries and PTSD, for which I had to jump through hoops to prove how far I could or could not bend, and be assessed for the disorder. Financially I was at a huge disadvantage after kidnap, rape, attempted murder, fraud and identity theft. Hearing that I needed to repay tens of thousands of dollars although there was proof of my conditions was enough to make me crave a drink, and since everyone around me drank, nobody really even noticed that I drank again. *Objects in the Rear View Mirror Are Closer Than They Appear.* Much closer. Like with my PTSD flashbacks, I was plunged back in time, into losing my way.

It took some time before I realized that going to a meeting and stopping again would help me to further my life, and would help me to help myself to pay back that debt that I truly felt I should not have, more than any glass of wine or intoxicated friend ever could. I got sober, and I rebuilt my entire life. I very literally went all the way from welfare to being successful and having wealth and investments, owning my own Sober Companioning and counseling corporation Danielle Delaney Counseling, Inc. (DDC, Inc.) and my production company for hosting, appearances and voiceover work Delangerous Productions(DelangerousProductions.com), maintaining my private practice, hosting my own show "The Real Deal With Danielle Delaney" on VoiceAmerica (to listen to my show and to hear what I'm doing now, visit www.ExpectDelaysBook.com) and earning both of my doctoral degrees and writing my book. I have so many other endeavors that I have yet to accomplish, and I know that I will reach every single goal. It was extremely far from an overnight success. With alcohol as my co-pilot, these things would not have been remotely possible, and that is an absolute truth. I could not have identified myself as a strong survivor and known what that meant. Now, I know who I am, and that I am no less a doctor and a counselor while I'm hosting a counseling radio show (www.voiceamerica.com/show/2552/the-real-deal-with-danielle-delaney) or while being a public motivational speaker and writer, and hosting and doing voiceover work. All of it is still me, being authentic and doing what I can to provide healing. All parts of my psyche and spirit grow with my intention and my work. Anything less than that is robbing myself of my future, and I found that working the Steps, Al-Anon, and SMART recovery and other holistic techniques helped me. There is no one-size-fits-all approach in my mind.

Prescription drugs are easy to misuse when you are traumatized. Many doctors will forget to tell you that, oh hey, grapefruit juice cancels out your antidepressants, in much the same way that antibiotics cancel out a birth control pill. Pretty useful, necessary and good things to know. Also important, drinking on antidepressants is like playing ping-pong with your brain chemistry. One drink is like two while you are on these meds; two drinks will hit you like four. Four will hit you like a ton of bricks. On and on. Some doctors dispensing meds for anxiety are meaning to hand you jumper cables, but they are tangled, and they are complicated.

Drinking or using any substance to "make you feel better" while on your journey to heal from any trauma at all is *Not A Through Street*. A wet road is a slippery road, period. In a fog, you need to see clearly, and this is not the way to your destination of healing. You need to *feel* this storm and utilize your own fog light, not go into a tunnel and hide. You may never come out on the other side if you operate in this manner. Actually FEELING your emotions will get you to the other side. You have to go THROUGH, not over and not around.

I recently saw an old video for Aretha Franklin's song "Think." I had no idea until my sobriety that the whole song is about caution and not driving drunk.

T H I N K.

Other than a bartender, nothing else will serve you now.

# Chapter 8

## DEAD ENDS AND EXITS

You may be totally miserable and afraid. Why wouldn't you be? You were victimized, traumatized, and given a very raw deal. You are unhappy and depressed and keep trying to get up. Why bother? Why not take the Exit?

You are WORTH IT, that's why. YOU are the reason that I am writing this book. I really don't have to! Do NOT allow your perpetrator and wrecking ball of a life event to win and demolish you.

So many obstacles and orange cones and warning signs. It may feel like it is just too hard. You wish the journey was over. You can't turn back, and you can't reverse.

Many trauma and rape survivors do commit suicide. Suicide Prevention is the only key if you have stopped here.

### CALL THE SUICIDE PREVENTION HOTLINE. 1-800-273-8255

This is a Dead End if you allow it to be. Do NOT. Your perpetrator(s) is/are not worth it!

You are correct. This is hard – not everyone has to travel this journey. You may have surrounded yourself with likeminded people with victim mentality who will cause you to swerve on your path. They can help you to go right off of a cliff with them. Steer away from them. *Far away*. It's okay! ***It is okay to outgrow unhealthy people!*** You can only see right in front of you in your headlights right now, but you can make the whole drive this way! It is enough; ***YOU are enough.***

You cannot get "there" from "here." You are not wrong. You are going to need to autocorrect. Do so. No permanent solution to a temporary problem will work. Keep going.

You may feel like your life is not within your control and is unmanageable. Your Light is dimmer every day. Suicidal Ideation is your constant Passenger. Your crisis is your constant Passenger.

It is a trick. It is a mindfuck. Language doesn't matter. You just have to steer. You have to control it before it spins you out of control. Jump start your Spirit. Go back, and go over these steps to reclaim your LIFE, your Light and your Soul. Do not allow them to win and to destroy and to wreck you. ***For what?*** Back out of this dead end, and far away from the exit ramp. You have too much living to do. You always have...keep going.

Nothing that you leave behind will be better than what is ahead. Nothing!

# Chapter 9

## DETOUR

In the darkness, it can be overwhelming to find your light.

It is there.

Make a change. Detour. Move if you have to, leave the familiar and go to a family member, a friend, somewhere new. The road you have been on may be leading you repeatedly to nowhere. If that is the case, raise your white flag and surrender. Ask for more help. It is a brave, strong, and unusual thing to ask for help. There are resources to help you; there may be friends and family willing and waiting to do so, as well. Reach. Go.

There are other paths, other routes, other lanes. Flag down some Soul Care Assistance. You are free. You are not in the trauma this moment. You are not married to this location where you live, this time period, this job, and this pain. It takes work and perseverance, but there are alternatives, and you have to seek them out.

Talk to your Counselor and Therapist about grounding techniques to keep you in the present time and in the moment. Visit www.Danielle DelaneyCounseling.com and www.ExpectDelaysBook.com so that I may lead you to further support and help you.

I can and do empathize with the search for the right treatment and modality, for the right health care professional to help guide you. I saw TWELVE, yes, twelve, therapists before I met Dr. Minton, who was life-changing for me. I suggested that we try some EMDR (Eye Movement Desensitization and Reprocessing) work which I had read about for trauma survivors, which is designed to help to alleviate some of the distress of traumatic memories. It really helped me. *HE* really helped me. I do find EMDR and a few other methods extremely illuminating in treatment.

I had been to see one Therapist who thought that discussing my sex life, my race, and my partner choices in the years leading up to my kidnap, rape and attempted murder was appropriate. Those are not factors in a crime of violence and have nothing to do with it. I had another who could not be on time, and suffering from PTSD and needing to drive only at certain times and living far from him was an issue when he was late. Yet another had opinions and thoughts about my assaults that were way off the mark. I wanted to give up, believe me...my small roadster was even run off of the road by an eighteen-wheel big rig truck that did not see me, and did not stop after my car was shoved into the freeway guardrail by his truck as I was on my way to a therapy appointment. I was badly shaken and afraid, but I rescheduled, got a rental car, and went to therapy. I made it my full-time job to do every-thing that I could to heal, and make my life better than this shell of what it had once been. Please go to www.expectdelaysbook.com for more resources that I provide to help you to find your way.

It is completely true that life is continuing to go on whether you participate in it, or not, all around you. Friends of mine were having children and at that time, at 37 or 38 years old a decade ago, I, too, thought I had better hurry up if this was something that I wanted for my future. Many friends still had expectations of me, to be present for their kids' birthdays as well as their own, and in their defense, I sure acted like I could keep up even though the expectation was really too much. Going to all of those showers and birthdays along with the normal pressures of society of what it believes you are "supposed" to do at certain ages had done a number on my mind. I thought at the time that it was necessary to have a child very soon. In reality, after what I had been through and was still going through, I was no better equipped to handle the task of raising another human being than I was to fly to the moon. However, I had heard from an ex-boyfriend who said he just couldn't duplicate the relationship that we had 8 years prior, that he had traveled the world and realized over those years and travels that I was the one woman that he loved and that he most wanted to be with forever and to create a family. I still had strong feelings for him although the relationship had been stormy and he had not been trustworthy in the past. I assumed that he had grown up.

We began to see one another again and began our relationship again, although it meant flying to and from LA to New York and back often, for both of us. We wanted to have a child and get married as soon as possible. I did become pregnant easily at 38. I was so excited, I bought little plastic toy babies to break the news to my fiancé as well as to my father. I put them in their iced teas over dinner to break the news in a novel way. I embraced this as my new future, making all of the plans that any new mother-to-be makes, and then I miscarried a few months later. I found out that this person I was going to marry was a complete fraud and had concurrently carried on relationships around the globe, and had said the same exact things to multiple women in multiple countries; oddly they all looked like they could be related to me, to make it even creepier. One had been pregnant with his child, as well. *This is actually called serial reproductive abuse.* This man hadn't become a better person since I had left him almost a decade earlier... he had only become a better liar. The discovery of such intense deception and the miscarriage were traumatizing, my hormones were causing huge ups and downs, I felt the double sting of betrayal and loss, and there are few support resources for miscarriage. The baby registry stores continued to send mail and email, not knowing that I had suffered this loss. Reminders of babies and of time marching on were everywhere. One of the women he also deceived in Norway became a dear friend and an excellent support, and we are still close friends. She could not believe that, knowing what I had just come through, he had chosen to put me through more pain with such crushing timing while I was working on career, fraud repair, physical therapy, and a brain injury and healing from assaults.

At the same time, I was being harassed by an old "friend" by email, saying that I owed her money, when I had proof and cancelled checks to show I had repaid the small loan a year earlier. She had become an addict and could not keep track of time or records, and was desperate for money. She accused me of being "fine" because when I went to see her in New York, I had participated in walking around the city, as my leg injuries were actually worsening. That trip had been a terrible idea, but I tended to have several poorly executed plans in the first year following the first violent attack. All of this was going on as I was just trying to "keep it together" and rebuild some sort of a life for myself. I mention this, because it is important to know that while it is necessary to rebuild your life, it does not need to be at warp speed or carelessly. Choose yourself first, and the rest will fall into place. You do not need false starts, painful toxic people, or more suffering in your life.

Difficult things will come up. People we love will pass away or become ill. My father had foot cancer at this time; my dog Charlie that I loved for 15 years died. Three dear friends perished in accidents, leaving me in shock and grief; two others died from cancer very suddenly. I felt as though the clouds would never lift and all I could see was directly ahead of me, to the next minute, to the next day. The urge to self-medicate and just sleep as much as possible was overwhelming. With perseverance, you can get to the next road, over the next hill. Life doesn't stop happening because you need to heal. Know this, and keep moving forward, slowly but surely.

This is not a simple process by any means. You just have to keep going, day after day, and it will improve. Continue with talk therapy, no matter what. You'll get there.

I honestly had no idea that in my life, the lives that I have the privilege and the honor to shape and to guide would not be those of genetic children. That is not something I even want for myself. I have the honor and satisfaction of helping and reaching countless lives instead, in my thriving career, and they are no less worthy or less deserving. I find it beyond fulfilling to counsel and guide and shape people's lives in this different and extraordinary way. I am exactly where I need to be, and I worked incredibly hard for it in more ways than one. My experience of overcoming, along with my education, training and degrees, have made me an expert in my field and I can think of no success more rewarding than helping others. My life is not conventional, but it is very full and content.

Detouring from this moment and from where you are may be the best thing that has ever happened to you. No more stalls. If you have been trying and trying, do everything again, and ask for more help and *switch* gears. You can do this. Accept the situation. A change will do you good. There will be disappointments and delays, and it's okay.

**Expect them.**

# Chapter 10

## MERGE

You are a Soul with a Body, not a Body with a Soul.

This vehicle that is YOU is still more than drivable. It's now a very valuable classic.

You can begin to integrate what happened to you into who you are *now*. You can merge your old identity and view of yourself with and into who you are currently. The "before" with the "NOW." The "After." The **YOU**.

This can be a smooth and clear gear shift with support on your side. Keep asking for and seeing different people for support; that is all I

am asking you to persevere and to do. Survive.
Accept help and assistance with grace and bravery because your Light is on. Keep working in this way, and you will find your Soul and your Spirit. They never left you.

No more "wrong way" signs will appear because you have already been there and you now know how to avoid them. You are emerging, as you are merging. Your Soul and Spirit, too, merge with you.

You have direction and you are moving forward. Speed does not matter, because forward is still forward.

Your life was dramatically altered by a wrecking ball. Demolition did happen, yet you can and will rebuild. You can navigate through the delays. ANY delays.

You anticipate, prepare for, and *EXPECT DELAYS*. For all of us, they are inevitable. Now, you have learned to slow down, to park. To wait. To heal.

You are different now, but the demolition is over. The crash and burn is over. Its time to completely reconstruct. *What do you have to lose?*

Heed the signs. Slow down... Children at Play. School Crossing. You are learning to play again, you are in the school of life, educating yourself. Nobody escapes it. We are all getting through this thing called Life.

Progress and drive. Get through the messy, chaotic construction zone with your hardhat firmly on, and your Spirit intact. You lived and you learned, through the deafening noise. You are now a shining and strong structure, flaws and all. Your Soul was broken down, but it was also broken open.

Your Light has returned. Rebuild.

Expect delays, but reclaim your Life, Light and Soul. Go forward and win your race. The black and white flags are madly waving you in. You win, and nobody can *EVER, ever* take it from you.

Survivor.

Sail though that finish line.

You will know where you are going when you see it. Keep your eyes wide open.

# ACKNOWLEDGEMENTS

I dedicate this book to each and every Survivor and Client, who have individually so very bravely shared their lives with me, and entrusted me with their darkest truths. Thank you for showing me my purpose. You know who you are.

First and foremost however, I must thank my mother, the one and only beautiful brilliant and talented artist/sculptor, Myra Delene Willard Williams, without whose never-ending support, advice, belief in me, and her tireless modeling for her children of the very best that there is in human nature, humanity, morality and elegance for me to try my best to emulate, it would not have been possible to survive and to thrive. You stun me, and everyone else who is lucky enough to know you. You are a fantastic mother and friend – in the same way that you weld, paint, mold clay and create and carve creative and marvelous images out of marble and alabaster slabs of stone, you helped me to recreate myself as only you could give birth to me again; and my Father, Dr. Richard Allen Williams, M.D., who also told me from the moment I landed on this Earth that I could do absolutely anything, and I have, because HE did so first, himself! Harvard, your history, your music and your groundbreaking mind and medicine run through my veins. I am so very fortunate to be your child. I also thank my siblings, Kelly Williams Ching & her husband Ernest Ching, La Rae Williams & her partner Mark Nakagawa, and Allen Williams & his partner Maarten van Himbergen, for being ever-present and for being the brilliant people that I am so very proud to call my family. I also dedicate this work to my nieces, Annalisa Simone Ching and Kelsea Taylor Williams. You are my everything, and both of you represent hope for the future generations. Never, ever give up! Please continue to use your voices and to stand up for what you believe! Thank you to my Aunt Estelle Waters for your wise, sage advice and support over the years and your example of caregiving as a talented, skilled and wonderful Nurse. I look up to you. I also thank the rest of my enormous extended family & cousins, Aunts and Uncles; the Willards and the Williamses, respectively, originally of Charleston, WV and of Wilmington, DE. Thank you to my grandmothers, Jessie Higgenbotham Willard Dorcas and Mildred Williams. We all come from some incredibly strong stock; thank you for always having my back. A special heartfelt thank you to my Uncle Ernest Willard, LICSW; without your careful guidance I might not be here, for my healing would not have been possible. Thank you also to Genita Evangelista Johnson, you are an inspiration to me; you are an uplifting, lovely, and welcome addition to my family, as is your extended family.

I thank **Ellen DeGeneres,** for the depth and wisdom that you shared with me about success itself...that random meeting through a mutual friend truly helped to shape my thoughts about my future, Ellen! **You have my endless respect and admiration**; VoiceAmerica Worldwide Talk Radio and my Executive Producer, the inimitable Sandra Rogers, Jeff Gerstl, and Deena Gonzalez, for being the best parts of the Network that believed in me the most and gave me an enormous platform from which to reach the entire world with my show; Dr. Barbara J. Young for being who you are and an inspiration, Todd Bridges for showing me by example and through friendship how to fearlessly share my story, as did he; Christina Adams for being the best Nurse on the planet as well as the very best friend and constant sounding board that I could ever have asked for in all my life.

Richard Taite for inspiring me in my field and by being a true and unique trailblazer; Chris and Pax Prentiss for being omniscient enough to know that I would be a sure bet for private Aftercare for hundreds of your clients; Jon Abeyta, my top-secret weapon for 30 years of your friendship, genius photography, and fierce makeup skills; a special thank you to Erica Spiegelman, for being the colleague by whom I am the most inspired and most "rewired"; see what I did there? Thanks to Angelica Bridges for being a true friend that has been unwaveringly there for me for decades and gracefully stood beside me through all things; Jim Michaels for your steady vote of confidence in me and for being a solid friend; Robert De Niro for your friendship and for showing me at only 25 years old that I am special, and that I command attention; as you know, I truly took it to heart; Deanna L. Tryon, Chief of Protocol of the City of Los Angeles and Silicon Valley for being present for me, speaking out for me, and for being vocal about what survivors deserve. I thank Robert Doig, CPA for helping me to stay the course and for your *priceless* and I do mean priceless advice; Dr. Thema Bryant-Davis for talking to me & for sending me your phenomenal book, which was lifesaving in my time of crisis.

Additional thanks for your support and/or inspiring words, deeds, or presence over the years goes to, in absolutely no particular order: Louis Gossett, Jr., Karen McIntosh-Hill and Montel Hill, Wendy Gosse, Darren Stein, The Squirrels, Cindy Guyer, Dr. Susan Allen, Triangolo Family Clinic, Dr. Daniel Minton, Valerie Hinton, Elan Carter-Price, Goldie Shortridge, Jennifer L. Carpenter, Matthew McConaughey, Paris Hilton, Todrick Hall, Juliana Bedig Beeman, Candice Greene, Carol & Jim Shogren, Chris Noth for giving me great advice about what offers and pursuits NOT to follow, Leah Daniels-Butler for showing me "how to put my arm" which I shared with Jennifer Carpenter with much success for her to follow, Paper Chase, Fotek, Aimee Barraza who is the best Concierge and a lovely human being, Catherine Townsend-Lyon and In Recovery Magazine, Inc. for featuring me, Rev. Katia Romanoff, Ph.D., Bishop, The Esoteric Interfaith Theological Seminary, Bel Air Church, Temple Beth Shalom, Artie Hawk, Barbara Wells, Gail Neuman and M2 Financial Services, Ross Remien, Ashley Rogers, Michael Shaner, Noah Rothschild, Brad Lamm, Nick Loeb, Scott Oakford, Wendy Bair, Aj Benza, Norena Barbella, Carl David Blake, Rona Lewis, Rajiv Uttamchandani and H.E.R. USA, Norbie Gregory, Danielle Brown, Jennifer McDougall, Lacee Dilmore, DeLisa Davis, Draven David Roche, Marion Meyer, Marisha Fradiue, Deni Tyler and

*Dr. Danielle Delaney, Th.D., D.D.*

Matt Sala, LACAAW, Barry Siegel, Richard Feldstein, Beverly Hunter, Stacy Long, Christine Carillo-Thomas, Clyde Rush, Kimberly Kilker Moger, Kelly Maglio-Lewis, Juniper Graham, Simon Cowell, Portia Di Rossi, Stedman Graham, Jamie Diehl and John Stewart, Kimberly Hightower, Victor Webb, Walter and Deesa Gause, Lynn Miller, Reza Paya, Brian Paya, Monica Airo, Laura Ratmansky, Audra Wise, Ian Webber, Syd Wilder, Lysa Nalin, Eileen Henry, Oprah Winfrey, President and First Lady Barack Obama and Michelle Obama, Dr. Terry Dubrow, Sheila Hamilton, Radio MD, Slash, Michael Gluck and Erica Gluck, Dr. Dale Archer, Paul Sorvino, Stephanie B. Brouse & Jessica Rose Brouse, Sylvia Anderson, Catharine and Jeffrey Soros and family, The late and beyond great Prince Rogers Nelson, The Beverly Hills Holistic Chamber of Commerce, Julie Brassington, Kim Lentz, Giles Harrison, Kelly Amor, Christina Schuch, Demi Moore, Doug Sherrod, Norm Aprahamian and Georgette and your sons and your Norm's 76 family and Wayne Michael Carter from Norm's 76, Brooke Butin of HeatherBrooke, Dena Mesler Klotz, Jo Davidson, Dr. Maya Angelou, Jaclyn Waterman and Dr. David Frey DDS and Stephanie Frey, Rachel and Gregory Yates, Margo Long, Zoley Byg, Yassmine Johansen, Shannon Powers, Stephanie Hauser, Valerie Penso and Adam Cuculich, Rose Miller, Jed Mottley, Robert Rosen, Roz Annengerg, Richard Annenberg, Valeska Grant and Will Occhi, Jane Velez-Mitchell, Marcellas Reynolds, Leonard Lee Buschel, Sheila from WeHo Station 8, Cedars-Sinai Hospital, Gavin de Becker and 'The Gift of Fear,' Anna Salter, Keith A. Somers, Gary Stuart, Catalina & John Fillipakis, Reesa Mallin, Johnnie Raines, Jason Wood, Erica Annenberg, Gunnar Nelson, TicTock Couture Floral, Eddie & Anna Zaratsian and Nelson Castillo, Gary Peskin and Rose's Agency, Ron & Stacy Edwards and Roberto Ysais, SoHo House West Hollywood and NYC and Malibu, Chris Aponte, Rachel Corbett, Evan Haines, Suzanne Drabek, Arlene Lerner, Jodie Foster, Pamela Sunderland, Taylor King and Espionage, Mike Freeman, Bobby Trendy, Carrie Gonzales, Emilio Estevez, Jeff Spenard, Matthew Barrackman, Wesley Idol, Robee Owens-Gill, Billy Riback, Carrie Stevens, Serria Bishop Tawan, Dr. Stephen Trudeau, Jeff Greenberg, Myrna Castanon, Bryan Altman, Mackenzie Phillips, Steve Guttenberg, Tyra Banks, David

Hinegas, the Zarian twins, Lawrence and Gregory, Women's Association for Addiction Treatment (WAAT), my BHS classmates and UCLA class-mates, Brittney Hinton and Brianna Williams, Dezetta Burnett, Marcia Belmont, Elliot Epner, John Kirby, Iris Klein, IT Models, Sanders Agency LTD., in Los Angeles and New York, Dorothy Day Otis Artists Agency, House of Pang Agency, PTI Agency, Shelley Pang, Danie Wulff, Pamula James, Wanda Reese, Samantha Reese, Sean Kanan, Carin LeVine, Jeryl Bryant, Jennifer Finnegan, Cara Goff, Yensa Werth, Iain Christianson, Lulu Vibert, Denisa Willhite, S & S Transportation, Airport Express and Rony Vadas, Tiffani Bova, Summer Altice, Elliot Mintz for helping me out of a rumor frenzy, the Lamas and Dahl families of Beverly Hills, CA, especially Izzy, Vicky and Alexandra, Charles Nelson Delaney, The Sexual Assault Crisis Agency, UCLA Rape Crisis, Verna Harrah Sexual Assault Examination Clinic, The Joyful Heart Foundation and Mariska Hargitay, Courtney Ahrens, California State University at Long Beach, The City of Long Beach, The Belmont Plaza Olympic Pool, City and County of Los Angeles Office of Protocol, DeLisa Davis, Maddie, Susie, Steve, Joann, Miss Chong, Evelyn Austin, and everyone at His and Hers Hair Goods Co., Robyn Barnett Block & Keith Block, Christopher Scott Pearson, Renee Appell, Jill Levy-Fisch, Marcia Beverly, Pat O'Brien, the City of Los Angeles for the beautiful backdrop for the street photographs that I've taken for this book, SAG-Aftra, the late Johnny Giosa, the late great Pat Ast, the phenomenal late Dr. Frank H. Ryan, and my very dearest departed Spencer Beglarian.

Thank you to you; *you*, who knows just how to soothe me and how to rest quietly beside me with music when I am weary, and who makes me feel that I can trust, feel cared for, be properly adored, and feel safe with you. You are both my VIP and my MVP.

You know *exactly* who you are.

Lastly, a giant THANK YOU to Raymond Aaron and to Cara Witvoet for listening to me, talking to me, encouraging me, and for pushing me to excel and to complete this book!

# ABOUT THE AUTHOR

Dr. Danielle Delaney, Th.D., is a Certified Crisis Intervention Counselor, specialist in Addiction & Recovery Aftercare, Rape Crisis Counselor, Spiritual Counselor, and is also a Sober Coach and an Interventionist. She also specializes in the area of Adults Molested as Children as well as LGBT issues and drug-assisted rape and survivors of domestic violence. Danielle works with individuals, families and couples seeking healing and resolution of their challenges, and helps them to more clearly see the path to their holistic wellness and to their higher selves. She hosts "The Real Deal With Danielle Delaney" on VoiceAmerica, the World Leader in Internet Media, on Tuesdays at 2PM PT.

Danielle Delaney has the distinction of being the youngest and the only woman of color to own a Sober Companioning business in the United States of America. She is soon to be featured in a "Top 50 Under 50" piece about American Female Entrepreneurs as well as appearing as a specialist in an upcoming documentary about healing and retraining the brain.

In addition to her work as a counselor and as an Interventionist with numerous inpatient facilities internationally, Danielle maintains her private practice in Hollywood, California and works with crime survivors with the Sexual Assault Response Team (SART) for The City of Long Beach and works as a State Certified court advocate. She works as a volunteer on the hotlines for suicide and rape. Her practice as a concierge counselor often involves going to the homes of high-profile individuals so that they may maintain their privacy whilst seeking help. Danielle can be found listed in Psychology Today. She is also a writer and is a contributor to numerous health journals including those for the Minority Health Institute, The Association of Black Cardiologists, and the National Medical Association, and has been filmed for a segment for the television series "The Doctors." "Expect Delays" is her first book, and she is presently working on her second. Danielle works with the boards of The One Wish Foundation and The Joyful Heart Foundation, and was on the Board of Directors for Dr. Frank Ryan's Bony Pony Ranch Foundation for at-risk youth. The County of Los Angeles Office of Protocol has hailed Danielle as a "proven asset to the City and County of Los Angeles." She has made numerous appearances on Radio MD, Rewired Radio with Erica Spiegelman, and has appeared on five-time Emmy award winner Sheila Hamilton's radio show in Portland, Oregon and on Dr. Barbara Young's syndicated international show, "Transformation For Success." Danielle's media, voiceover work and appearances can be found under Delangerous Productions. She will be launching her International Sobriety and Recovery Lifestyle Brand of clothing in 2017.

Danielle is being featured in In Recovery Inc. Magazine for the "Strong Women in Recovery" special Issue for Fall 2017. Dr. Delaney has been named Director of the H.E.R. USA Conference for International Humanity Education and Rights, in Los Angeles for September of 2017. She will also be a headlining speaker at the Conference.

Danielle holds a bachelor's degree in Psychology from UCLA as well as doctorates in both theology and divinity, and has earned additional certifications and degrees from the Sexual Assault Crisis Agency in Orange County and the Esoteric Interfaith Theological Seminary. As a survivor herself, she is uniquely qualified to understand and assist her clients. Through her work and contributions, Danielle is dedicated to assisting people in affecting enduring & beneficial changes in their lives and in making sense of the chaotic world around them.

To contact Dr. Danielle Delaney, please go to
www.ExpectDelaysBook.com
www.DanielleDelaneyCounseling.com or
www.DelangerousProductions.com

For additional content, bonus materials, and updates on the Expect
Delays App, go to www.ExpectDelaysBook.com